JEWELS FROM JAMES
A DEVOTIONAL COMMENTARY

George Carman

Published by **CARMAN BOOKS**
8413 Cactus Flower Dr.
Ft. Worth, Texas 76131
www.carmanbooks@att.net

"Jewels from James"
Copyright © 2013
George Carman
All rights reserved

ISBN 978-1492703402

Cover design by Dale Carman

All rights reserved. No part of this book may be reproduced in whole or in part without written permission from the author, except by a reviewer who may quote brief passages in a review; nor may any part of this book be reproduced, stored in a retrieval system, or transmitted in any form or by any means electronic, mechanical, including photocopying, recording, or other, without permission in writing from the author, except as provided by USA copyright law.

Scripture quotations are from the *ESV® Bible (The Holy Bible, English Standard Version®)*, copyright © 2001 by Crossway Bibles, a publishing ministry of Good News Publishers. Used by permission. All rights reserved.

Published by **CARMAN BOOKS**
8413 Cactus Flower Dr.
Ft. Worth, Texas 76131
www.carmanbooks@att.net

Published and bound in the United States of America

SECOND EDITION: SEPTEMBER 2013

TABLE OF CONTENTS

Preface

1	Introduction And Author, James 1:1	1
2	Facing Trials Victoriously, James 1:2-11	11
3	Facing Temptations, James 1:12-18	23
4	Hearing And Doing The Word, James 1:19-27	37
5	Impartiality Towards All, James 2:1-13	49
6	Relationship Of Faith And Works, James 2:14-26	59
7	Faith Without Works Is Dead, James 2:14-26	69
8	Dangers Of The Tongue, James 3:1-11	79
9	True And False Wisdom, Learning The Difference James 3:13-18	89
10	Fighting And Wars Among You, James 4:1-12	101
11	Boasting About Tomorrow, A Different Lifestyle, James 4:13-17	113
12	Warning To The Rich And Patience In Suffering, James 5:1-12	123
13	The Power Of Prayer, James 5:13-20	133

DEDICATION

This book is lovingly dedicated to my father, Charles B. Carman. He was a great bible class teacher, a faithful Christian and he served as an elder in the church. His favorite book was the book of James. I am proud to be his son and I know he would have enjoyed reading my *Jewels from James*.

ACKNOWLEDGEMENTS

I want to express my sincere appreciation for the dedicated work done by my sister, Karen Jinkerson. She spent numerous hours proofreading this book. She not only made needed corrections to the grammar and spelling, but she also offered many good insights and modifications that provided more clarity to the contents of this book. Her help was invaluable.

I also want to my thank my son, Dale Carman, for designing the fabulous cover of this book. He is a talented designer and a very busy man. I appreciate him for taking time out of his schedule to create such a magnificent cover design for *Jewels from James*.

I want to thank the Sunset International Bible Institute, my alma mater, for the wonderful Bible training they provided me over the years. They taught me how to properly respect the word of God and they provided me with the tools I needed to spend a lifetime studying and teaching the Bible. SIBI is a tremendous place to learn the word of God.

Finally, I want to thank my wife, Hilda, for her patience with me while I was writing this book. She allowed me to spend countless hours in my study without complaining. She also patiently listened to me as I talked about the contents of this book. Hilda is a faithful companion who has traveled all over the world with me as I taught the word of God. She is a most precious *"jewel"*.

PREFACE

When my father, Charles Carman, died in 2002 I determined to write a commentary on the book of James in honor of his life and because of his great love for this particular New Testament book. Now, eleven years later that promise has come to fruition.

I, too, love the book of James. It was one of the first books I taught after graduating from Sunset International Bible Institute. The ragtag notes from that original class are a part of what has become this book. *Jewels from James* is a devotional commentary. By that I mean my book is not weighed down with Greek words and difficult phrases. It is a book meant to edify and enlighten the reader whether they are a new Christian or a longtime member of the Lord's body.

My intention is to present the book of James in a way that analyzes the meaning of the book to the people to whom it was written and then to provide some practical applications to those of us who are living in the 21st Century. My purpose is to encourage us to absorb the spiritual truths contained in this great book so that we might grow in faith, in Christian character, and in zeal to serve the Lord.

The Bible is the inspired word of God. My book is not. As you read *Jewels from James* I would encourage you to have your Bible close by your side. Keep your finger on the word of God as you read this commentary and you will have a better chance to understand the meaning correctly.

This book is the first volume in a series called *Into the Word Series*. The Lord willing, volume two will come out soon. It will be entitled *Love Letters from John*, It will be a devotional commentary on the epistles of John.

Happy reading! I pray God will grant you the wisdom to understand His word, the faith to believe it, and the courage to do what it says.

Dr. George Carman, 2013

Chapter 1

INTRODUCTION AND AUTHOR

James 1:1

"James, a servant of God and of the Lord Jesus Christ, to the twelve tribes in the Dispersion: Greetings."

James is a small book with only five chapters and one hundred and eight verses. That is three verses less than the Sermon on the Mount! (Matthew 5:1-7:29) Although it is a short New Testament book it is filled with practical and useful suggestions on how to live a better Christian life. A study of this portion of scripture will definitely impact the life of everyone who takes to heart the wonderful teachings it contains. Many refer to James as the *"Proverbs of the New Testament"*.

In our study we will use the English Standard Version (ESV). So, if you have an ESV Bible available, please read it at least once during your study. Of course, you may prefer to use your own study Bible and that is perfectly all right. However, it would be to your advantage to read from different versions of Scripture each time you read through the book of James. Doing so will give you added insight into its meaning. It is suggested that you read all five chapters at one sitting. It won't take that long. It would be good for you to read the entire book at least 3 times during the time it takes you to read this commentary. In addition, read the entire section of Scripture contained in each chapter of this study guide. That will serve as an extra reading.

Do not underestimate the value of Bible reading. You will be blessed if you don't take shortcuts. This book provides you with many verses that support the points being made. Some of the quotations contain only the portion of the text that applies to the topic being discussed by James. Other passages are mentioned merely for your reference. To receive the most benefit from your study, have your Bible handy and read all of the references that are given in every chapter of this devotional commentary.

In order to get a good start on your study why not stop right now and read the book of James in its entirety . . . Wasn't that easy? We are now ready to begin our study.

LEARN THE ABBREVIATED OUTLINE

There are many good authors who have written detailed outlines on the book of James. If you have other resources, by all means, look them over to find the outline you like the best. This author likes short outlines that can either be memorized or written in the margin of one's Bible. By doing so, you can pick up your Bible, turn to the book of James and immediately be reminded what to expect as you study the book. Here is the outline I use in my personal study.

JEWELS FROM JAMES

Chapter One:
Facing trials and temptations victoriously, 1:1-18
Hearing and doing the word, 1:19-27

Chapter Two:
Impartiality towards all, 2:1-13
Faith without works is dead, 2:14-26

Chapter Three:
Dangers of the tongue, 3:1-12
True and false wisdom, 3:13-18

Chapter Four:
Fighting and wars among you, 4:1-12
Boasting about tomorrow, 4:13-17

Chapter Five:
Warning to the rich and patience in suffering, 5:1-12
The power of prayer, 5:13-20

MEN NAMED JAMES

There were several men named James in the New Testament. Three of them were very influential in the early church. Which one wrote the book of James and when did he write it? Read on to discover the answer.

JAMES, THE SON OF ZEBEDEE

This man was an early disciple of Jesus and later became an Apostle. As you probably know, he was the brother of John and a fisherman by trade, Matthew 4:21-22. His father, Zebedee, apparently owned a family fishing business. It is thought that Salome was his mother. This is based on a comparison of Matthew 27:56 to Mark 16:1. It was while he was working at his trade that Jesus called him to become a fisher of men, Mark 1:16-20.

The son of Zebedee, was executed by King Herod Agrippa I around 41 A.D. as recorded in Acts 12:1-2. Because of his early death it is unlikely that James, the son of Zebedee, wrote the book of James. King Herod Agrippa I only appears once in the New Testament. He was born about 10 B.C., the son of Aristobulus and Bernice. About 5 B.C. Herod the Great killed Aristobulus because he feared he was trying to take his throne.

Agrippa I was the grandson of Herod the Great, the King who reigned when Jesus was born. It was Herod the Great who killed the little children as recorded in Matthew 2:16-18. King Agrippa I was the brother of Herodias, the woman who asked for the head of John the Baptist on a platter in Matthew 14:6-8.

Herod Agrippa I was sent to Rome after his father died and was educated there. He became friends with Gaius, the grandnephew of the Emperor Tiberius. Gaius eventually became Caesar and took the name Caligula. Emperor Caligula honored Agrippa I by conferring upon him the title King and gave him the territory previously held by both Philip and Lysanias. When Claudius became Caesar of Rome, Agrippa I was re-confirmed as King. This was about 41 A.D. This re-appointment gave Agrippa I extreme power and liberties that many other rulers in the Roman Empire did not enjoy. Because he had such power this evil man took it upon himself to kill James, an Apostle of the Lord Jesus Christ.

The death of Agrippa I comes shortly after the execution of James, Acts 12:20-25. To learn more details about his death, read the account recorded in the writings of Josephus. He speaks of a slow agonizing death brought about because the King took on himself the glory that belonged only to God Himself. Thus Josephus confirms the account given by Luke in Acts chapter twelve. James, the son of Zebedee's early death makes it very unlikely that he was the author of the book of James.

JAMES, THE SON OF ALPHAEUS

He was also an Apostle of Jesus, Matthew 10:2-4. Little is known about this man. Church legend says he preached in Persia and that he died by crucifixion. There is not adequate evidence to support the theory that James, the son of Alphaeus, was the author of the book of James. This leaves us with one other option.

JAMES, THE BROTHER OF THE LORD

While many deny that Mary had other children, the Scriptures clearly show that she did. Mark 3:31-32 says, *"And his mother and his brothers came, and standing outside they sent to him and called him. And a crowd was sitting around him, and they said to him, "Your mother and your brothers are outside, seeking you."* The names of our Lord's siblings are listed in Matthew 13:55-56. They were James, Joseph, Simon and Judas (Jude). Jesus also had at least two sisters who are unnamed. Acts 1:14 informs us that Mary and Jesus' brothers were among the crowd of 120 meeting in Jerusalem when Matthias was chosen to replace Judas Iscariot as an Apostle of Christ. The margin of the ESV, in Acts 1:14, uses the plural of the Greek word *"adelphoi"* (translated brothers) referring to Jesus' siblings. Clearly, Mary had other children besides Jesus.

Some authorities identify him as James the Less while others give this title to James the son of Alphaeus. We do not know for sure. According to history James was beaten and stoned by the Jews and had his brains dashed out with a fuller's club. He died around 62 A.D.

Most conservative scholars credit James, the brother of the Lord as the author of the book of James. This author also believes the brother of the Lord Jesus Christ wrote the book of James.

DATE OF THE BOOK

Some would date the book as late as 62 A.D., the year of James' death, but this author prefers to date the book sometime between 45-50 A.D. It was probably written sometime before the Jerusalem Counsel of 50 A.D., Acts 15:1-35. Dating biblical books is not an easy task. One reason for giving James an early date is the contents of the book. In James 1:1 we learn the recipients were the 12 tribes in the Dispersion. In addition, James 2:2 speaks of the rich who came to their assembly. In the Greek text the word translated *"assembly"* is the word Synagogue. Early Christians often met in the Jewish Synagogues.

You can learn more about how dating is accomplished by researching good books that deal with the authorship and dating of Biblical books. One such book is *"New Testament Introduction"* by Donald Guthrie, Inter Varsity Press. There are also many in depth commentaries that deal with dating problems. Look at some of them and see what they have to say.

MORE ON JESUS' BROTHERS

Unfortunately, the brothers of Jesus did not totally believe in Him during His lifetime. Their lack of faith is clearly stated in John 7:5. Perhaps their doubt is the reason Jesus, while hanging on the cross, committed His mother, Mary, to the care of John, the son of Zebedee, John 19:26-27.

The resurrection of our Lord convinced his doubting brothers that He was the Christ, the Son of God. In Acts 1:13-14, as already noted, we learn that after Jesus ascended into heaven the Apostles, along with the women, including Mary, the mother of Jesus, and his brothers met together in Jerusalem for prayer. Evidently the brothers of Jesus were now firm believers that Jesus was all He claimed to be. Two of those siblings, James and Jude, authored New Testament books.

THE CHURCH LEADER AND AUTHOR

Before long, James, the brother of the Lord, emerged as a church leader and an elder for the church at Jerusalem. Five New Testament passages chronicle his rise to prominence in the early church, Acts 12:17; 15:13-21; 21:18; 1 Corinthians 15:7, and Galatians 1:19. Read each of these passages and learn what they say about this godly leader. James, like all the other biblical writers, wrote by the inspiration of the Holy Spirit, 2 Peter 1:20-21. Inspired means *"God breathed"*. Therefore, every word in scripture is holy and God given. The book of James does not contain man's words but the words supplied by the Holy Spirit of God. *"All scripture is breathed out (inspired) by God"*, 2 Timothy 3:16.

The Old Testament authors credited their message as being from God with statements like, *"Thus says the Lord"*. Similar statements appear thousands of times in the Old Testament. Paul wrote, *"If anyone thinks that he is a prophet, or spiritual, he should acknowledge that the things I am writing are a command of the Lord,"* 1 Corinthians 14:37. Peter calls Paul's writings *"scripture"* in 2 Peter 3:16. Yes, James was the human author but the words he wrote came from God through the Holy Spirit.

THE PROBLEM SOLVER

As an elder in the Jerusalem church, James played a prominent role in helping solve the problems recorded in Acts 15:1-35. The issue had to do with circumcision and keeping the Law of Moses. Certain Jews wanted to require Gentile Christians to be circumcised and to keep the Law of Moses, Acts 15:5. Those who held this view were called Judaizers. The Apostles and the Jerusalem elders met to discuss this issue in order to come to a God approved decision. James authored a letter to the Gentile Christians informing them the decision of the church leaders. Gentile Christians were not required to be circumcised or to keep the Law of Moses as claimed by the Judaizers. They were saved by faith and obedience to the Gospel just like the Jewish believers. You can read his letter in Acts 15:23-29.

A UNIQUE SERVANT OF THE LORD
James 1:1

"James, a servant of God and of the Lord Jesus Christ, To the twelve tribes in the Dispersion: Greetings."

Jesus' brother was a very humble Christian. It is very interesting to me how James did not identify himself as the brother of the Lord. Instead he identified himself as *"a servant of God and of the Lord Jesus Christ"*. What would **YOU** have said had you written the book of James? I fear that if it had been me, I would have said something like this, *"George the brother of Jesus Christ – **and don't you forget it.**"*

Look at James 1:2 to learn that he called the recipients of his letter *"brothers"*. The Greek word translated *"brothers"* is used in many places to indicate brothers and sisters (siblings) as already mentioned. The footnotes of the English Standard Bible help to clarify the meaning. It tells us the New Testament usage is as follows: *"The plural Greek word adelphoi (translated 'brothers') refers to siblings in a family in New Testament usage . . . depending on the context, adelphoi may refer either to men or to both men and women who are siblings (brothers and sisters) in God's family, the church."*

It is important to note that James calls his relationship to Jesus to be one of a *"servant"* but when he speaks of his relationship to his fellow Christians he calls them *"brothers"*. For the author to call his fellow believers *"brothers"* and His fleshly brother *"Lord"* is a true indication of his humility. It would be good for us to increase our awareness of brotherhood among believers.

When I was doing mission work in Chiang Rai, Thailand I purchased a daily English newspaper. Consequently I came to know the proprietor very well. One day I went into his store with my Thai co-worker, Thui, walking alongside me. The storeowner asked me who my friend was and I replied, *"He is my brother".* The proprietor asked, *"Oh, did you have the same mother?" "No",* I replied, *"We have the same Father".* This incident provided me with an opportunity to explain just what I meant by calling my Thai co-worker a brother. What a blessing it is to be able to consider our fellow Christians as our brothers and sisters!

CONCERNING HUMILITY

Our first *"jewels"* are on the topic of humility. Knowing the characteristics of humility will help us to be more like our brother, James. **DEFINITION: Humility**, *"lying low; brought down, humble, of low degree, lowly".*

FIRST JEWEL: The servant of the Lord is to be humble. *"Clothe yourselves, all of you, with humility toward one another, for God opposes the proud but gives grace to the humble,"* 1 Peter 5:5. How are you dressed? Are you clothed with pomp and pride or with the clothing of humility? Be careful lest God oppose you because of your pride. Pride could be defined as the opposite of humility. Pride means *"rising excellency".* Unchecked pride will lead us to destruction, Proverbs 16:18.

SECOND JEWEL: True humility requires submission. *"Submit yourselves therefore to God,"* James 4:7. How different is that from pride? The Bible also says, *"Humble yourselves, therefore, under the mighty hand of God so that at the proper time he may exalt you, casting all your anxieties on him, because he cares* *for you,"* 1 Peter 5:6-7. Submit yourself to God and humility will follow. Read Luke 18:9-14 for a lesson from Jesus on humility. It is the story of the publican and the Pharisee. Jesus' conclusion commended the publican with these words, *"Everyone who exalts himself will be humbled, but the one who humbles himself will be exalted,"* Luke 18:14. True humility requires submission not only to God but also to each other, Ephesians 5:21.

THIRD JEWEL: Trust that God will care for you. We worry too much about earthly things and the necessities of life. We should put all of our cares into God's capable hands. The humble person puts his full weight upon God as the one in charge of his life and as the giver of all good things, James 1:17. Read the words of Jesus in the Sermon on the Mount to learn a lesson about putting your full trust in God for the necessities of life, Matthew 6:25-34. True humility requires that we give up our anxiety and trust God to take care of our needs.

FOURTH JEWEL: The humble will be exalted. God will exalt His humble servants in due time, *"God opposes the proud but gives grace to the humble,"* James 4:6. Jesus said, *"Whoever exalts himself will be humbled, and whoever humbles himself will be exalted,"* Matthew 23:12. Like James, we need to be humble servants of the Lord.

WHAT IS A SERVANT?

The word *"servant"* comes from the Greek word *"doulos"* and means *"bond-servant, slave"*. In our country we don't like the idea of being a slave to anyone. Yet, Jesus described Himself as a bondservant. Do you remember the time when Jesus' Apostles were seeking prominent places in the Lord's kingdom? Read Mark 10:35-45 to be reminded of the time when James and John, the sons of Zebedee, came asking Jesus to give them prominent positions when He set up His kingdom.

Jesus not only rebuked the idea of trying to obtain leadership roles based on the worldly pattern but He also taught them the proper track to greatness in the kingdom of God. World leaders are at the top being served by the masses working under their authority. This is not the kingdom paradigm. Our Lord came not to be served but to serve. We who are being served by the Savior must also be servants to others. How different is that from the worldview?

James identified himself as a servant of the Lord. We have already seen that he did not emphasize being Jesus' brother. That is because he knew that Jesus was more than a brother. He was the Savior, the King of kings and the Lord of lords. This humble man was following in the footsteps of Jesus by being a servant. We need to learn that lesson too!

THE RECIPIENTS OF THIS LETTER

James wrote to the twelve tribes in the dispersion. The idea of the dispersion (scattering of the Jews) has several meanings. It is a term used to designate the Jewish nation that was scattered all over the known world. This scattering of the Jewish race was partially a result of the carrying away into captivity as recorded in the pages of the Old Testament. According to the Bible, the reason for that National dispersion of Israel and Judah was their sins, Jeremiah 9:16. Even after the return from Babylonian captivity during the time of Ezra and Nehemiah many Jewish people chose to remain in the countries and cities where they lived.

The Dispersion also included people who moved away to live in another country as a matter of personal choice. Over the course of time this type of scattering happens to all Nations. Hence, the term *"Dispersion"* originally consisted of Jews who were living in cities outside of the Promised Land who kept the teachings and customs of the Jews while living among the Gentiles.

In the New Testament the term Dispersion might also refer to Jewish Christians who were scattered among the nations. Read Acts 2:5-12 to see a list of the Jews who were part of the Dispersion who came to Jerusalem from many nations in order to worship on the Day of Pentecost. Some of them became believers and stayed in Jerusalem for a long while. It is likely that some of those who became Christians that day eventually went back to their adopted homeland.

Finally, Acts chapter eight tells us of another Dispersion. After the death of Stephen a great persecution against the church began in Jerusalem. It was so severe that most of the believers living in Jerusalem were scattered to other cities. *"Those who had been scattered preached the word wherever they went"*, Acts 8:4. The congregation in Antioch was established by some of those believers, Acts 11:19-21.

Therefore, we conclude that the book of James was written to Jewish Christians living outside of Jerusalem during the First Century. His writing greatly blessed them as it will bless any people who study his book, regardless of the Century in which they live.

DISCUSSION QUESTIONS:

1. Discuss the three men named James and discuss which one wrote the book of James. Give the reasons for your choice.

2. Discuss the siblings of Jesus and discuss what you know about them.

3. What position did James, the brother of the Lord hold in the Jerusalem church? Was he an Apostle?

4. Discuss the recipients of this book and give your understanding of who they were.

5. What important letter did James write to the Gentile Christians and where is it located in the Bible?

6. Define the word servant and discuss ways we can serve.

7. Define humility. How does James 1:1 indicate the humility of the author?

8. Discuss the four *"jewels"* found in this chapter that describe humility.

Chapter 2

FACING TRIALS VICTORIOUSLY
JAMES 1:2-11

James 1:2-4
"Count it all joy, my brothers, when you meet trials of various kinds, ³ for you know that the testing of your faith produces steadfastness. ⁴ And let steadfastness have its full effect, that you may be perfect and complete, lacking in nothing."

WHEN TROUBLES COME

This section provides us with spiritual teaching that can lead us to joyful recovery from the burdens that trials and tribulations bring to our lives. When life seems unfair, read James chapter one. There is no doubt that life on earth can become very difficult. The question is not *"if"* trials and tribulations will come to our lives – The question is *"when"* will they come. The most important question is: *"How will we handle the trials we face in life?"*

FACING MEDICAL DISASTERS

Slowly she walked back to her car with her head hung low. *"How could this be?"* she asked. The doctor had just instructed her to get her house in order because she only had six months left to live. The cancer was too far along. There was nothing else that could be done. *"Woe is me!"* the woman thought. *"How could this be happening to me?"* *"How could God let this happen to me?"*

FACING ECONOMIC DISASTERS

Yet another person, a man and the family breadwinner, was driving home with his thoughts in disarray. *"How can I tell my wife?"* he thought. *"How will we be able to survive?"* He expected to be working for his company for the rest of his career. He loved his job and looked forward to going to work each day. Today, however, his boss informed him that due to cutbacks, he was out of a job. *"It isn't fair,"* he moaned. *"I have been a faithful Christian for years. How could God do this to me?"*

FACING RELIGIOUS PERSECUTION

Still another man was in dire straits after being confined to a jail cell. He was not a bad person but here he was sitting in a dingy jail cell. The reason for his arrest was not because he had been a thief or a murderer but because he allowed brethren to meet in his home in order to worship the God of heaven. *"What did I do to deserve this?"* he asked. *"Where is the God of Abraham, Isaac, and Jacob?" "All I did was meet to worship my Lord and look at me now!" "How could God allow this to happen to me?"*

We sometimes think religious persecution only happened during the First Century. However, even as you read these words, many believers living outside of America's shores are being persecuted because of their faith in God and the Lord Jesus Christ! There are countries where church buildings have been torn down and the wood confiscated by Government forces. Many others have been arrested and put in jail simply because they met to worship God on the Lord's Day!

These illustrations are just a few examples of the problems that occur in the lives of many Christians in our *"modern"* world. Indeed, there are many bad things that happen to good people. You probably know someone who has suffered severe trials in their life. Maybe it is you yourself that has been put through a furnace of affliction. What *"jewels"* does James have to offer us in the face of our trials and tribulations?

What are Christian people to do when things go wrong? It is difficult not to react in a negative way to the problems of life. That is one of the reasons God inspired James to write his book. He offers us inspired insights on how to react when things go wrong. The inspired author does not seek to solve the problem for us, instead he teaches us a spiritual approach to difficulties that will give us a positive mindset when we find ourselves in difficult situations. As a child of God we learn how to smile through the tears! How different is that from the ways of the world.

COUNTING TRIALS AS PURE JOY!
James 1:2

"Count it all joy, my brothers, when you meet trials of various kinds."

In this first section we will learn the need to have a positive attitude towards troublesome times. We are taught to have a different perspective on life than people of the world. This new joyful attitude will prevent troubled souls from having a pity party when things go wrong. Instead, they will learn to rejoice in the Lord.

We need to understand that all people, both good and evil, have problems in life. As Christians, we learn how to handle things differently than those outside the body of Christ. The principles found in the book of James will help us to do just that. It will help us learn not to spend too much time searching for an answer to the question, *"Why me?"* In a more proactive way, the child of God counts it all joy when trials come because he knows, at the proper time, God will provide a good outcome. He also realizes that troubles mature the believer in a way that good times cannot do.

Being a believer does not exempt us from being tested. All humans must learn to navigate through the bumps and bruises this world has to offer. Sometimes it seems like Christians suffer even more than those who have no faith in Christ whatsoever. We should not be puzzled by this fact. The book of Job shows us clearly that even the best of God's children are sometimes put through very severe trials. When bad things happen to us we need to trust God to carry us through no matter what happens to us. Peter wrote, *"If you suffer as a Christian, do not be ashamed, but praise God that you bear that name,"* 1 Peter 4:16. Therefore, whether we suffer physical or spiritual trials, we should count it all joy.

Most people just don't count difficulties as joy. All too often, people claiming to have faith in Christ respond to trials just like people who have no religious beliefs whatsoever. To consider something as pure joy means to look forward to the event that is coming up with delight or gladness.

Joy is usually found when people experience a pleasing situation. Let's face it. It is easier to find joy in good times than it is in bad times.

Here are a few things that bring me joy:
- Catching the eye of my true love.
- A newborn baby. (Especially one of my own.)
- Having Grandchildren.
- Receiving honest praise.
- Seeing a loved one or friend after a long absence.
- Watching my favorite team winning a championship.
- Eating my wife's pot roast. (If you ever experience that treat, I guarantee it will bring you pure joy too!)
- Finishing a worthy project.
- Reading my Bible and teaching the word of God.

Did you notice anything missing from my list? There was no mention of trails and tribulation in my list of joyful events. Have you ever listed your troubles so you could accentuate them with expressions of godly joy? James teaches us to face trials of many kinds with an attitude of joy. How can we do that? Where is the pleasure in living through terrible ordeals?

When Paul, the Apostle, spoke of his thorn in the flesh, he asked God to remove it from him three times. God said, *"No, my grace is sufficient."* Therefore, the Apostle accepted God's response with delight. He wrote, *"For the sake of Christ, then, I am content with weaknesses, insults, hardships, persecutions, and calamities. For when I am weak, then I am strong,"* 2 Corinthians 12:10. It would be good for us to stop and list some of the major difficulties we are currently experiencing, and spend some time trying to find joy in them. Yes, that is a difficult task but it is part of the maturing process.

GAINING UNDERSTANDING

Too many people misunderstand the difficulties of life. They think God is punishing them for their sins. Other people seem to think they are so bad that they deserve to be punished. Others, like Job, think they are being punished unjustly. Job thought that somehow God made a huge mistake! The first thing he did was to have a pity party. *"Why was I born?"* he asked, Job chapter three. For a while, he even wondered if God was his enemy. At other times he had the idea that if God would just come down and talk to him everything could be straightened out. For most of the time during his affliction Job found no joy in his suffering. He, like us, wanted to know *"why?"*

Is there an answer? We may never know the total picture as to why we suffer so many difficulties, but we can gain some good information on how to turn our attitude into one of joy.

BENEFITS GAINED THROUGH SUFFERING
James 1:3-4

"For you know that the testing of your faith produces steadfastness. ⁴ And let steadfastness have its full effect, that you may be perfect and complete, lacking in nothing."

James helps us to find joy by providing five *"jewels"* we can gain through our trials and tribulations. Knowing the benefits we can receive provides a giant step towards finding joy in suffering.

FIRST JEWEL: A faith that is tested (proven). It is one thing to claim to have faith in God but it is entirely something else for our faith to stand firm and even to grow when things go wrong. Ask Abraham, Genesis 22. God told him to take Isaac, his only son, the one whom he loved, and offer him as a sacrifice on Mt. Moriah.

The faith of father Abraham was so strong that he was willing to offer Isaac on the altar as a human sacrifice because he believed if he did so God would bring Isaac back to life. In spite of the difficulty he faced, Abraham still believed God would make of him a great Nation through Isaac his son, Hebrews 11:17-19. Trials truly do test our faith! After Abraham's faith was tested, God provided an animal for the sacrifice and saved Isaac from death, Genesis 22:13.

The trying of our faith is accomplished when we pass through the crucible of suffering. It is likened unto gold passing through the fire, 1 Peter 1:7. True faith grows stronger when it is put to the test. For this reason, my brothers, count it all joy when trials come your way.

SECOND JEWEL: It develops steadfastness. The Greek word translated *"steadfastness"* in the ESV bible is translated by the word *"patience"* in some translations. The meaning of this Greek word is, *"to stay under; steadfast; to bear up under; to hold out"*. Steadfastness (patience) comes when we endure trials. As the level of our steadfastness increases so does our ability to handle the trials that come our way. When we pray for patience, it could well be that God will answer our prayer by sending difficulties our way. So, my brothers, count it all joy when you suffer the trials of life.

THIRD JEWEL: So you may be perfect (mature). The word perfect means to be *"complete; mature; of full age"*. It never means sinless perfection. Many excuse their sinful behavior by saying *"No one is perfect"*. To be perfect in the biblical sense is somewhat like fruit maturing on a tree. The fruit comes in different shapes and sizes. The fruit may have a bird peck or a bruise on it, but it is still mature. That is, it is ready to eat. The word translated *"perfect"* always means to be mature or full-grown. You can have a few bumps and bruises and still be mature. So, my brothers, count it all joy when trials come; it will help you to become mature in the Lord.

FOURTH JEWEL: It makes you complete. The word *"complete"* means to be *"whole in every part"*. Paul wrote, *"Now may the God of peace himself sanctify you completely, and may your whole spirit, and soul and body be kept blameless at the coming of our Lord Jesus Christ,"* 1 Thessalonians 5:23. We can never be *"whole in every part"* without experiencing troubles and tribulations. So, my brothers, count it all joy when troubles come, because when you have endured you will be made whole. That is to say, you will become a more complete child of God.

FIFTH JEWEL: It causes you to lack for nothing. I remember some years ago buying an insurance policy on my house. The agent gave me a packet of information that included a form upon which I was to make a list of everything in the house. This list was important in case a burglar came and stole some of my possessions. The paper exhorted me to make a complete list so that I would lack for nothing in the event I needed to make an insurance claim. Trials and tribulations give us the ability to lack for nothing (spiritually speaking). The list that ensures completeness is a tried faith, an increase in steadfastness, and to be mature (perfect). So, my brothers, count it all joy when troubles come, because they will help you achieve a spiritual position where you lack for nothing.

These five *"jewels"* should rank very highly among the good things Jehovah does for His children. It is an amazing thing that our Lord uses difficulties, trials, and tribulations as a way to make us stronger in Him. Read 1 Corinthians 10:13 to learn that even when we are undergoing difficult times God is in control. He will not permit us to be tempted beyond what we are able to bear. With His help, we will not only overcome our problems but we will become a better person because of them. I heard someone say, *"This too shall pass!"* as he reflected on his current difficulties. *"After all"*, he explained, *"this world is not my home. I'm just passing through on my way to my heavenly home."*

GAINING WISDOM
James 1:5-8

"If any of you lacks wisdom, let him ask God, who gives generously to all without reproach, and it will be given him. ⁶ But let him ask in faith, with no doubting, for the one who doubts is like a wave of the sea that is driven and tossed by the wind. ⁷ For that person must not suppose that he will receive anything from the Lord; ⁸ he is a double-minded man, unstable in all his ways."

THE RIGHT APPLICATION OF KNOWLEDGE

Now that we know *"why"* we should count it pure joy when trials come our way let's turn our attention to the *"avenue"* by which we gain the insight we need to cope with the problems of life. In the context of James chapter one, wisdom provides the avenue that gives us the ability to count it all joy when we *"meet trials of various kinds"*.

It is important to understand this truth. When you are puzzled by problems, ask God for wisdom to handle things correctly. He will grant it to you when you ask in faith without doubting. No doubt God gives a measure of wisdom to each individual when he is born. He gives more wisdom to some people than He does to others. Even so, an increase in godly wisdom only comes from the Lord and is only available to those who ask for it.

Wisdom is defined as *"cleverness, skill, the right application of knowledge"* It is man's responsibility to gain the knowledge. We do this by means of study and research. It is always hard work. Learning the Word of God has no shortcuts. It takes time and effort. The wisdom to rightly use the knowledge we gain comes from God through the avenue of prayer. God is a gracious and giving God who delights in giving His children those things they ask of Him in faith, Luke 11:11-13.

KINDS OF WISDOM

There are two kinds of wisdom in this world. We must learn to discern between godly wisdom and worldly wisdom. Worldly wisdom comes from man. Worldly wisdom often looks and acts like the genuine article but it is false. Notice the words of the Apostle Paul, *"the world through its wisdom did not know him, God was pleased through the foolishness of what was preached to save those who believe,"* 1 Corinthians 1:21. There are many who think they are wise who are devoid of any spiritual wisdom whatsoever. Intelligence does not always equate to wisdom. Neither does grey hair. The worldly wise have great learning but they often deny God, our Creator. Many educated wise men also deny that Jesus is the Christ and do not believe He rose from the dead. While it is good to receive a good education do not be confused. True spiritual wisdom comes from God not from a professor in an institute of higher learning. We will continue our study of the two kinds of wisdom when we study James 3:13-18.

ACQUIRING WISDOM

James 1:5-8 describes the process we must go through if we are to gain spiritual wisdom. Follow these *"jewels"* to learn how to gain it.

FIRST JEWEL: Recognize your need. Do you lack wisdom? The first step is to realize your need for godly wisdom. If you don't feel the need it is doubtful that you will ask for it. Without wisdom you cannot develop into the faithful well-rounded Christian the Lord would have you to be.

SECOND JEWEL: Ask God. When Solomon was a young King he prayed for wisdom rather than long life and riches. God was well pleased with his request and granted him wisdom plus great riches and honor, 1 Kings 3:3-15. The Lord our God loves to go above and beyond what we ask or think, Ephesians 3:20-21. The avenue for asking for wisdom from God is prayer, 1 John 5:14-15. James 4:1-2 teaches that sometimes we fail to receive because we don't ask. Other times we fail to receive because we ask incorrectly. As you receive knowledge of God from His word don't forget to ask Him for the wisdom to use it.

THIRD JEWEL: Know that God gives according to our faith. A person must believe God will do what He has promised. Be like Abraham. He was *"fully convinced that God was able to do what he had promised,"* Romans

4:21. When you ask be persistent with a faith that does not waver. You can know that the Lord will grant your request for wisdom. Since we must ask in faith it would be advisable for us to increase our faith by a study of the word of God, Romans 10:17.

FOURTH JEWEL: Do not doubt. Read Mark 9:14-29. This passage describes a father with a demon-possessed son. The Apostles could not cast the demon out because of their lack of faith. Since the Apostles didn't believe they could do the job they couldn't. As he saw Jesus descending from the mountain the father turned to the Lord for help. The Lord asked him if he believed He could cast the demon out. The father responded, *"I believe. Help my unbelief!"* Mark 9:24. Do not doubt God's promises. If you do, you will fail.

Our text, James 1:6-8, compares the doubter to a wave of the sea that is blown and tossed by the wind. Such a person is unstable and will receive nothing from the Lord. He is a double-minded man (literally means *"double souled"*) and is unstable in all his ways. I wonder how many of our prayers go unanswered simply because we doubt? God has the ability to give good gifts to His children, James 1:17. However, when we doubt, we destroy any possibility of an affirmative answer.

Knowing Scripture can often make one appear to be filled with wisdom but that is not necessarily true. Even Satan can quote scripture, Matthew 4:5-6. Gaining knowledge is man's part and giving wisdom is God's. True godly wisdom comes in direct response to the prayers of those who ask in faith with no doubting. *"For that person must not suppose that he will receive anything from the Lord; he is a double-minded man, unstable in all his ways,"* James 1:7-8.

THINGS DO EQUAL OUT
James 1:9-11

"Let the lowly brother boast in his exaltation, ¹⁰and the rich in his humiliation, because like a flower of the grass he will pass away. ¹¹ For the sun rises with its scorching heat and withers the grass; its flower falls, and its beauty perishes. So also will the rich man fade away in the midst of his pursuits."

I remember playing a game of golf with one of my friends. On the first hole, I was on the green in regulation (two strokes). I fully expected to par the hole. Instead, I four putted for a double bogey! If you play golf, you know how disgusting that can be. I left the green muttering to myself about how unfair the game of golf was. On the back nine, I one putted four greens in a row. That is exceptionally good for me. As my playing partner and I walked to the next green, he commented on my putting prowess and said, *"In golf, things have a way of evening out"*. That is exactly the lesson James teaches us in chapter 1:9-11. That is, things have a way of equaling out.

It seems likely that James wrote this section to explain how fairly life turns out for those who love the Lord and obey His will. Our troubles may seem unfair at the time, but in the end, things will even out. Therefore it matters not if we are rich or poor. If we love God we will receive the reward He promised to the faithful. It also seems that James is teaching us that when death comes both the rich and the poor stand on equal ground. We will all die and we will all be judged according to the deeds we have done, whether good or evil, 2 Corinthians 5:10.

LIFTING THE POOR AND HUMBLING THE RICH

FIRST JEWEL: Lifting up the poor, James 1:9. God lifts up the poor and honors them when they are people of great faith. Consider the poor widow who cast her entire substance (two small copper coins) into the treasury while Jesus and His disciples looked on, Luke 21:1-4. Jesus said, *"I tell you the truth, this poor widow has put in more than all the others. All these people gave their gifts out of their wealth; but she out of her poverty put in all she had to live on"*. This clearly shows us that our contribution to God is weighed by the sacrifice that was made and not by the amount of money offered. On the Day of Judgment things will definitely equal out. The poor will be lifted up and the rich will be brought low. Things do have a way of equaling out.

SECOND JEWEL: The rich will be humbled, James 1:10. Wealthy Christians should take pride in their *"humiliation"*. Well now, what does that mean? It seems that James is letting the rich know that their wealth does not guarantee exaltation in God's eyes. The Lord will not take away the troubles of life nor will He remove the sting of death just because one is wealthy. It does not matter if one is rich or poor, one day he will stand before the judgment seat of Christ. The only question is *"Were you faithful with what was entrusted to you?"* That looks like equal treatment to me.

THIRD JEWEL: The frailty of life, James 1:11. This text compares human life to the grass of the field or to a flower in full bloom. Because of the scorching heat they both wither and die. So is the rich man in the midst of his pursuits. Solomon pointed out *"that the living know that they will die,"* Ecclesiastes 9:5. The Hebrew writer informs us that *"man is destined to die once, and after that to face judgment,"* Hebrews 9:27. Can you see how things even out? All men, both rich and poor, will stand on equal footing when they present themselves before the Christ. Once again, the question is, *"Have you been faithful?"*

ILLUSTRATING EQUALITY

Consider this. A poor man lives his life on earth and endures many hardships. He learns about the Lord and he becomes a Christian. Yet, he is still poor. His hardships still remain. However, now he is *"rich"* in faith. He realizes how unimportant the trials of life are when compared to the day God will grant him eternal life. His former difficulties become nothing when compared to the crown of life the Lord promised to give him one day.

A rich man also lives on this earth and prospers. He has everything his heart desires. He also hears the Gospel and obeys it. He lives on this earth with all of the luxuries that riches bring to a man. However, he, too, is a person with many troubles. He realizes that many of his problems cannot be solved by his wealth. He uses his blessings in a way that helps others and pleases the Lord. He, too, dies. He stands before the Lord on the same basis as the poor man just mentioned. Because he did not trust in his riches and because he was generous with the wealth God gave him, he too, receives his reward. Just like his *"poor"* counterpart he hears the words, *"Well done, good and faithful servant".*

One is lifted up and another is brought low. Both receive their reward. Things equal out for both of them. That is another good thing about God. He always does the right thing in His dealings with mankind. James truly equips us to face trials victoriously. He points out the benefits we can receive through suffering. He also shows us the avenue to receive wisdom from God. James helps us learn how to count our trials and tribulations with all joy.

DISCUSSION QUESTIONS:

1. Discuss the difficulty of considering trials of all kinds with joy.

2. Discuss the five benefits *"jewels"* gained through suffering. Which one is more difficult for you and what can be done to increase that attribute?

3. Define wisdom. Discuss our ability to recognize people who have godly wisdom. What should we look for? See 1 Kings 10:6-9.

4. Discuss worldly wisdom and the benefits it gives to us. What is the downside of worldly wisdom?

5. Is there any value in worldly wisdom? If so, name some of them.

6. Discuss the four *"jewels"* listed for acquiring wisdom.

7. Discuss the relationship of knowledge and wisdom.

8. James 1:9-11 expresses the fact that all things equal out. Discuss what that means and how it works out equally.

Chapter 3

FACING TEMPTATIONS
JAMES 1:12-18

James 1:12

"Blessed is the man who remains steadfast under trial, for when he has stood the test he will receive the crown of life, which God has promised to those who love him."

THE GLORIOUS CROWN

This chapter begins by pronouncing a blessing upon the person who endures trials to the very end. Such a person will receive a victor's crown. The word *"blessed"* is a word that means happy. Jesus spoke of this kind of happiness in the Beatitudes, Matthew 5:1-12. For example, the Lord said, *"Blessed* (happy) *are the pure in heart, for they shall see God,"* Matthew 5:8. We already learned from James 1:2 to *"count it all joy . . . when you meet trials of various kinds."* The one who remains steadfast under trials will be amply rewarded. This verse also applies to people who endure temptations to sin.

FIRST JEWEL: God crowns His faithful servants. Won't it be grand to receive a victory crown? God promised this reward to those who demonstrate their steadfastness in the face of life's trials. When we endure, we will receive a crown. The word for crown is the Greek word *"stephanos"*. This type of crown was a wreath or circlet placed on the head of a King. It was also worn by victors in athletic games and by generals who were victorious on the battlefield. This word, *"crown"*, is used to describe the reward we will receive when we finish the good fight of the faith. It is not a jeweled crown but a victory wreath. It is only awarded to those who endure to the very end. I am looking forward to my crown! How about **YOU**?

SECOND JEWEL: God's promised reward is for those who love Him. In this verse, James mentions love for the very first time. Love serves to motivate us to steadfastness in the face of trials. What better motivation for faithfulness than love? Paul revealed that prophecies, tongues, and knowledge would pass away. In contrast he said, *"faith, hope, and love abide"*. Of the three he declared love to be the greatest, 1 Corinthians 13:13. Jesus Himself taught that love is the greatest commandment, Matthew 22:36-40.

Job expressed his love for God when he said; *"though He slay me, I will hope in him,"* Job 13:15. Such a statement could only come from the heart of a person filled with such love for God that it could not be quenched by the trials he was going through.

John taught that love for God compels us to obey His commandments, 1 John 5:2-3. God has a precious *"jewel"* in store for those who love Him: a victory crown. Don't give up! Stand firm in your faith and in your love for God. Faith provides the basis for enduring and love provides the motivation to remain faithful until death.

FACING TEMPTATIONS
James 1:13-15

"Let no one say when he is tempted, "I am being tempted by God," for God cannot be tempted with evil, and he himself tempts no one. 14 But each person is tempted when he is lured and enticed by his own desire. 15 Then desire when it has conceived gives birth to sin, and sin when it is fully grown brings forth death."

As great as the promised crown of life is there are many obstacles standing in our way. Becoming a Christian does not mean we will no longer face temptations. The truth is the devil seems to redouble his efforts once a person turns to God. Temptations will come to us throughout our lifetime. Sadly, too many Christians fall to the temper's allurements and fall back into sinful practices. To remain in a fallen condition will cost a person his soul.

EVEN JESUS WAS TEMPTED

Immediately after His baptism by John the Baptist the Holy Spirit drove Jesus into the wilderness to be tempted by the devil, Mark 1:12-13.

Because our Lord emptied Himself and was born as a man, He had no choice but to suffer temptations to sin just like every other human being. After His temptations were over we learn that *"he* (the devil) *departed from him* (Jesus) *until an opportune time,"* Luke 4:13. Doctor Luke lets us know that Jesus was tempted many times during His lifetime.

Later in His ministry, Jesus called Peter *"Satan". "Get behind me, Satan! You are a hindrance to me. For you are not setting your mind on the things of God, but on the things of men,"* Matthew 16:23. Satan often uses people to serve as his agents in tempting others. If satan tempted Jesus throughout His ministry why would we think our circumstances would be any different? Are we to be spared when our Lord was not? Most certainly the devil will tempt us too! Satan is compared to a roaring lion and we are warned to be careful lest we become his next meal, 1 Peter 5:8.

TEMPTATION IS NOT A SIN

Jesus, our great High Priest, was *"in every respect tempted as we are, yet without sin,"* Hebrews 4:15. If the act of being tempted were a sin, then our Lord was a sinner. But, Jesus overcame every temptation the devil had to offer. How great is that? What a tremendous Savior is Jesus Christ our Lord! He achieved something no other human has ever achieved and that was a sinless life. An important truth we can learn from Jesus' temptations is to be tempted to sin and to actually sin are two entirely different things.

LEARNING ABOUT SIN

It is because we are creatures of choice that we are so prone to sin. Our weak faith and our pride often lead us astray. *"Let anyone who thinks that he stands take heed lest he fall,"* 1 Corinthians 10:12. It sure didn't take Adam and Eve long to sin did it? Cain followed in the steps of his parents and became the first murderer. Every living soul that has lived to an age of accountability has sinned and fallen short of the glory of God. *"There is none righteous, no not one,"* Romans 3:10. Everyone has sinned with the exception of Jesus Christ our Lord.

WORDS DESCRIBING SINFULNESS

Sin: Means to *"miss the mark"*. This word is explained by the imagery of an archer shooting an arrow at a target and missing it altogether. He may go too far, or too short, or he may miss the target on one side or the other.

The word sin is sometimes used in a broad sense to cover every kind of wrongdoing. For example, the Bible says, *"All wrongdoing is sin,"* 1 John 5:17.

Transgress: This word is defined as *"one who steps aside or goes aside from"*. To transgress is to go beyond what is written. Many scriptures warn us against the sin of going beyond the written commandments of the Lord. Moses wrote, *"You shall not add to the word that I command you, nor take from it, that you may keep the commandments of the LORD your God that I command you,"* Deuteronomy 4:2. To add to God's word is to transgress.

Omission: This word describes the person who does not go far enough in carrying out God's commandments. Iniquity, our next word, can also describe the person who sins by omission. We dare not omit any of the commandments the Lord has given us. Omission of God's commandments was the reason King Saul was rejected by the Lord. Read 1 Samuel 15:1-34 to learn the details of King Saul's disobedience.

Iniquity: This word is used in Isaiah 59:1-2 along with the word sin. The Greek word most often translated by the English word *"iniquity"* means: *"non-observance or transgression of the law whether unknown or willfully violated; lawlessness."* All lawlessness is iniquity.

Blasphemy: This word means, *"to drop evil or profane words, revile God or divine things."* It often carries the idea of malicious slander. The Jewish scribes accused Jesus of blaspheming in Matthew 9:1-7. In this passage Jesus forgave the sins of a paralytic before He actually healed him. *"Some of the scribes said to themselves, "This man* (Jesus) *is blaspheming,""* Matthew 9:3. The real blasphemers were the Jewish leaders who accused Jesus of doing his miracles by the power of the devil, Mark 3:30. Their sin was the sin of blasphemy against the Holy Spirit, a sin that never has forgiveness. Read Matthew 12:22-32 and Mark 3:22-30 for more details. Other forms of blasphemy can be forgiven but not the sin of blasphemy against the Holy Spirit. The wisest course of action is to never revile or speak evil of God or divine things.

WINNING THE BATTLE

In our Christian life we may not win every battle, but we need to put forth every effort to strive against sin, even unto the shedding of our blood (death), Hebrews 12:4. When we do sin, we need to repent of our wrongdoing and confess our sins, 1 John 1:9. He is faithful and just to forgive us through the blood of His Son, Jesus Christ. *"My little children, I am writing these things to you so that you may not sin. But if anyone does sin, we have an advocate with the Father, Jesus Christ the righteous. He is the propitiation for our sins, and not for ours only but also for the sins of the whole world,"* 1 John 2:1-2. God provides a way for us to make our life right with Him by acknowledging our wrongdoing as set forth in scripture.

How did our Savior defeat the devil? Did he call a legion of angels to come and help Him? Did He call upon God to miraculously move Him to a safe place? No, the Lord did not use miraculous power or Divine privilege to defeat satan. The Lord used Scripture to refute the evil one. We must do the very same thing if we expect to defeat the devil when he tempts us. David wrote, *"I have stored up your word in my heart that I might not sin against you,"* Psalm 119:11.

WAYS TO DEFEAT SATAN

FIRST JEWEL: Know the Scriptures. This is a surefire way to defeat the tempter. It is the method Jesus used to defeat the enticing temptations the devil presented to Him in Matthew 4:1-11.

SECOND JEWEL: Resist the devil and he will flee from you, James 4:7. The Greek word translated *"resist"* means *"to stand against, to set one's self against, to withstand, oppose"*. Looks like a fight to me. As strong and evil as the devil is he cannot defeat the person who takes his stand on God's word. Thus says the Lord will win every time.

THIRD JEWEL: Flee from the devil. There are two areas where the child of God is instructed to run away from the conflict. It would be foolish for us to try to stand when God has instructed us to run away. What are the things we are to run away from?

Flee from idolatry, 1 Corinthians 10:14. Nothing is worse for a believer than idolatry. The example of Israel in the Old Testament shows how God felt when His people were unfaithful to Him. Consider the words of Jeremiah the Prophet, *"Why has the LORD pronounced all this great evil against us? . . . Because your fathers have forsaken me, declares the LORD, and have gone after other gods and have served and worshipped them,"* Jeremiah 16:10-11. Graven images are not the only form of idolatry. In Colossians 3:5 we learn that covetousness is idolatry. Anything we put in the place that belongs to God is our idol. Run from idolatry. Run as fast as you can!

Flee from fornication, 1 Corinthians 6:18. The sex drive is very strong so when you are tempted with sexual sins run for your life! Sexual activity is a privilege of marriage, Hebrews 13:4. God will judge fornicators and adulterers. Jesus delivered a needed lesson when He said, if a man lusts after a woman he has already committed adultery in his heart, Matthew 5:27-30. In like manner, a woman can sin by lusting after a man. Run from sexual sins. Run as fast as you can!

FOURTH JEWEL: Stay out of the devil's reach. As mentioned earlier, Peter likens the devil to a ravenous lion seeking to devour his next meal, 1 Peter 5:8. If you hang around with the wrong people, the *"lion"* will eat you up. *"Do not be deceived, bad company ruins good morals,"* 1 Corinthians 15:33. Just as spoiled fruit that rests against the good fruit will ruin the good, even so bad companions will destroy good people. I never saw a good apple make a spoiled one good but I have certainly seen the opposite!

I see the lion (the devil) as being staked to a pole by a powerful chain. If we stay outside the length of the chain we won't be hurt. However, if we step too close and somehow find ourselves inside the area of his domain he will devour us. Don't be deceived; the devil has much power. There are times to fight and times to run for you life! Realize that the fight against evil is ongoing and the destiny of our souls is at stake.

TAKE PERSONAL RESPONSIBILITY FOR SIN
James 1:13

"Let no one say when he is tempted, 'I am being tempted by God,' for God cannot be tempted with evil, and he himself tempts no one."

We will now learn two important truths when it comes to sin. Both of them are based upon the need for each individual to realize his own personal responsibility. *"The soul who sins shall die. The son shall not suffer for the iniquity of the father, nor the father suffer for the iniquity of the son . . .the wickedness of the wicked shall be upon himself,"* Ezekiel 18:20.

FIRST JEWEL: Don't pass the blame to others, James 1:13. Don't blame God for your sins because *"He cannot be tempted by evil and he himself* *tempts no one".* Don't fall for the lie, *"the devil made me do it."* Eve made the mistake of blaming satan but God did not accept her excuse. Adam made the mistake of blaming the woman, but God did not accept his excuse either. Who, then, should we blame? We have no one to blame but ourselves. Every person is responsible for his own sins.

SECOND JEWEL: Accept personal responsibility for your sins. Accepting personal responsibility is different from accepting the blame for our actions. A person can admit he did wrong and still deny personal responsibility to correct his wrongdoing. When we don't acknowledge that we have done something wrong, we cannot be brought to repentance. Accepting personal responsibility for our deeds means we are willing to take whatever steps are necessary to get right with God. *"If we confess our sins, he is faithful and just to forgive us our sins and to cleanse us from all unrighteousness,"* 1 John 1:9.

When King David faced the reality of his sin with Bathsheba, he humbly acknowledged his error with these simple words, *"I have sinned against the Lord,"* 2 Samuel 12:13. Read Psalm 51 to see all that David wrote after his sin with Bathsheba. He expressed sorrow for sin and gave a humble confession of wrongdoing. Accepting personal responsibility for our sins like King David will bring us back to God. Upon repentance we will receive forgiveness and the restoration of our soul.

STEPS THAT LEAD TO DEATH
James 1:14-15

"But each person is tempted when he is lured and enticed by his own desire. ^{15} *Then desire when it has conceived gives birth to sin, and sin when it is fully grown brings forth death."*

James clearly outlines the disastrous process that leads us to spiritual death. I am calling these steps *"jewels"* but they must be considered as negative jewels because they tell us things we should not to do rather than the things we should do. Knowing them will help us to know the steps that lead a person into a state of sinfulness.

FIRST JEWEL: We are enticed. Our evil desire entices us to do what is wrong. This particular Greek word translated *"entice",* means *"to catch by bait".* Can you visualize the scene? A man sits on the riverbank with a fishing pole in his hand. At the end of his line is a hook made of steel. He covers the hook with bait making it appear to be food to the fish. The fisherman plops his line into the river waiting for a fish to take the bait. Before long the line jerks and a fish is caught. The poor fish will never swim the river again. The fish that was seeking food has become food for the fisherman. It is all right to bait a fish, but please don't do it to people!

Watch out! The devil loves to cover up sin with enticing bait that makes wrongdoing look very attractive. Once we take the bait we will be eaten alive by our sinful actions.

SECOND JEWEL: Desire conceives and gives birth to sin. We must learn to deal with temptation before we conceive an evil deed in our heart. Sin, once conceived, will likely give birth to sin. If we are alert we can abort the temptation to sin before it gives birth to sin. However, it would be better not to allow our sinful actions to lead to conception in the first place. When sin is allowed to become fully-grown it will kill us. That is the nature of sin. Once we are enticed to take the bait iniquity is conceived in our hearts and gives birth to sin. Our actions, when left unchecked, will bring us to a disastrous spiritual condition.

THIRD JEWEL: Sin brings forth death. Sin is a killer of the soul. God warned Adam and Eve of the consequences of sin when He said, *"in the day you eat of it* (the forbidden fruit) *you shall surely die,"* Genesis 2:17. In Genesis 5:5 we read, *"All the days of Adam were 930 years"*. But God told him he would die on the very day he sinned. Did Jehovah change His mind? No, He did not! Adam and Eve died spiritually on the very day they ate of the forbidden fruit.

The Apostle Paul calls this the law of sin and death in Romans 8:2. From the time God gave Adam and Eve this law they became responsible to God for their actions. The law is very simple; if you sin you die. The book of James reaffirms the truth that full-grown sin brings forth death. In some cases the sinner dies physically but in every case he dies spiritually. That is the consequence of full-grown sin. It brings forth spiritual death.

JESUS SETS US FREE!

It is only through the sacrifice of Christ Jesus that we are set free from the Law of Sin and Death, Romans 8:2. This freedom begins with the new birth as Jesus informed Nicodemus in John 3:1-7. Read Romans 6:1-18 to receive a better understanding of the process of the new birth. When a person, by faith, is baptized into Christ, he experiences a new birth. This new birth takes place when, by faith, we obey the Gospel. We are born into Christ's kingdom when we are baptized into Christ.

Baptism is in the likeness of the death, burial, and resurrection of Jesus Christ. As Jesus died so we also die to sin. He was buried in the tomb and our old man is buried in water. As He rose from the dead so we are raised to walk in newness of life. What a graphic picture of the new birth! It is through this process of faith and obedience that we become dead to sin and alive to Christ.

When Christians sin they do not need to be baptized again but they do need to confess their sins and ask for forgiveness. How wonderful that our God is a God of second chances! Without his grace and mercy we would all surely perish!

THE EXAMPLE OF ACHAN – Joshua 7:1-26

The teaching found in James is well illustrated by the story of Achan, the son of Carmi, the son of Zimri. We read about him in Joshua chapter seven. Israel had just entered the Promised Land and were preparing for battle against the city of Jericho. You know the story. Israel marched around the walls of the city once a day and on the seventh day they made seven trips around the city walls. The priests sounded their trumpets, the people shouted loudly, and the walls of Jericho fell down giving Israel the victory. They were given the victory by the hand of God Himself.

Because it was the first city to be taken after crossing the Jordan River, it was declared to be a devoted city. That meant the spoils belonged to the Lord and not to the people. No one was allowed to take any of the plunder for themselves. Usually the army took the spoil and divided it among the participants. God commanded this city to be different. The spoil was to be devoted to God who would give them the victory.

Certainly no wise General would march around a city for seven days and expect the walls of the city to fall down giving them the victory. This battle belonged to God and to God alone. The city of Jericho was devoted to the Lord. The people of Jericho, both young and old were to be destroyed along with the livestock. All of the gold, silver, bronze, and iron were to be dedicated to the treasury of the Lord.

However, Achan saw some very valuable items in the ruins of Jericho. He saw a Babylonian robe, 200 shekels of silver and 50 shekels of gold. Perhaps he looked to the right and then to the left and saw no one there. Perhaps he looked to the front and then to the rear and saw no one looking. *"I am safe",* he thought, so he took the items and hid them in his tent. From the events that follow we learn his family was aware of what he had done. They shared in his guilt and were stoned to death right alongside Achan.

As a result of Achan's sin, God was displeased with all of Israel. There are some sins a child of God commits that cause innocent people to suffer severe consequences. The church cannot prosper when some in their number disobey the clear commandments of the Lord.

The next city to be destroyed was a tiny city named Ai. There is no mention of prayers being offered to God for guidance before the Israelites left for battle. That was a leadership error. This over-confidence contributed to a serious defeat for the people. Only a few warriors were sent to Ai but Israel was soundly defeated in the battle and thirty-six people died.

Joshua was confused and downhearted because of this defeat and he fell with his face to the ground until evening. God promised Joshua that Israel would be victorious against their enemies but here they were, soundly defeated. Joshua did not understand and he feared the people of Canaan would rise up and destroy all of Israel. God said to Joshua, *"Get up! Why have you fallen on your face? Israel has sinned . . . they have taken the devoted things,"* Joshua 7:10-11. When there is sin in the camp God's people cannot win the victory.

Joshua, following God's lead, cast lots to discover that Achan was the guilty party. Achan admitted his sin. *"It is true! I have sinned against the LORD, the God of Israel. This is what I have done: When I saw in the plunder a beautiful robe from Babylonia, two hundred shekels of silver and a wedge of gold weighing fifty shekels, I coveted them and took them. They are hidden in the ground inside my tent, with the silver underneath,"* Joshua 7:20-21. As a result of his sin, Achan and his entire family were stoned to death. Don't turn a blind eye to sin in your family. God may well hold you as guilty as the sinful family member.

TEMPTATIONS ACCORDING TO JAMES

We see (are tempted)	-	Satan's action against us
We are enticed (desire)	-	An appeal to our sinful nature
Evil desires conceive	-	Sin takes hold of us
Gives birth to sin	-	Sinful desire develops
Full-grown sin brings death	-	Consequences of sin

ENJOY GOD'S GRACIOUS GIFTS
James 1:16-18

"Do not be deceived, my beloved brothers. ¹⁷ Every good gift and every perfect gift is from above, coming down from the Father of lights with whom there is no variation or shadow due to change. ¹⁸ Of his own will he brought us forth by the word of truth, that we should be a kind of firstfruits of his creatures."

In this section, we learn the nature of true goodness. To fail to recognize the source of all good things is to be deceived. This particular Greek word *"deceived"* means, *"being caused to wander or to be led astray"*. The King James Bible translates it by the English word *"err"*. The word is especially used of doctrinal errors, or religious deceit. Therefore for one to fail to recognize that God is the source of all good things is a doctrinal error and, consequently, a sin.

Every good thing we enjoy is a gift from God. Far too many people think they are enjoying the good life because of their own talents. Perhaps they have forgotten who it was that gave them all of their wonderful abilities. Everything we enjoy is a gift from God. It is His grace and great benevolence towards us that grants us the successes we enjoy. Thank you God for being the giver of every good gift. Help us, Lord to acknowledge You as the source of the blessings we enjoy.

PHYSICAL BLESSINGS

There are two kinds of blessings we receive from God. We receive physical blessings and spiritual blessings. Of course, the spiritual blessings far outweigh the physical. However, isn't it easy to dwell upon the physical blessings and to forget the spiritual ones?

Even as I write I hear the gentle sound of rain falling outside my window. Yes, even something as simple as a rain shower is a gift from God. Everything we have, including our ability to make a living, all of our belongings, and our families are gifts from the Father of lights. They come from a consistent giver who does not change like shifting shadows. Thank you, dear Lord, for being so consistent in a world of inconsistencies.

SPIRITUAL BLESSINGS

FIRST JEWEL: He gave us birth by the word of God. Read Psalm 19:7-11 and 119:97-105 to see the preciousness of the God's word. Through the word we learn what God would have us to do in order to be saved. Through the word we learn about Jesus the Messiah. Through the written word of God we have hope. Oh! There is so much more the word gives to mankind. The scriptures are such a wonderful blessing!

SECOND JEWEL: He made us the firstfruits of all He created. The idea of being the firstfruits brings to mind the commandment God gave Israel to bring the firstfruits of their crops and animals and dedicate them to the Lord. Read Exodus 13:11-16 and Numbers 18:12 for a brief look at this topic. In addition to crops and animals the firstborn son also needed to be redeemed to the Lord. In the Old Testament all the firstfruits had to be holy and without blemish.

In the Christian age the idea of firstfruits can be applied to everyone who is a Christian. *"They* (Christians) *were purchased from among men and offered as firstfruits to God and the Lamb,"* Revelation 14:4. The Apostle Paul well described this blessing when he wrote, *"Because God chose you as the firstfruits to be saved, through sanctification by the Spirit and belief in the truth. To this he called you through our gospel, so that you may obtain the glory of our Lord Jesus Christ,"* 2 Thessalonians 2:13-14.

Our righteous status is accomplished for us by the sacrifice of Jesus Christ and His blood. It is not because of our goodness but because of the goodness of God. He chose us and cleansed us from our sins. When we are obedient to His word He pronounces us to be among His firstfruits. As a child of God you belong to the Lord and are among a host of others who are in the very same place of honor. God is truly the giver of all good gifts. *"Of his own will he brought us forth by the word of truth, that we should be a kind of firstfruits of his creatures".*

Why would anyone think that God is not the giver of all good things? Why not make a list of your many blessings and offer a prayer of thanksgiving to the Lord? Thank you Lord for loving us and giving us so many wonderful blessings!

DISCUSSION QUESTIONS:

1. Describe the kind of crown God has in mind for those who remain steadfast under trial. Who in the Roman world wore this kind of crown?

2. Explain the difference between trials and temptations. Is it a sin to be tempted to do evil?

3. Discuss the five words for sin discussed in this chapter. Give an illustration of each.

4. Discuss the ways we can defeat the devil.

5. Discuss the two *"jewels"* from James 1:13 and explain how they are different.

6. Describe the steps that lead to death (3 *"jewels"*).

7. Name two kinds of blessings. Name your favorite from both kinds of blessings.

8. Discuss the teaching of the Bible that says we are the firstfruits to God and the Lamb. You may have to go to the Old Testament to give clarity in this discussion.

Chapter 4

HEARING AND DOING THE WORD
James 1:19-27

James 1:19-21

"Know this, my beloved brothers: let every person be quick to hear, slow to speak, slow to anger, ²⁰for the anger of man does not produce the righteousness that God requires. ²¹Therefore put away all filthiness and rampant wickedness and receive with meekness the implanted word, which is able to save your souls."

ACHIEVING A GODLY TEMPERAMENT

James now addresses our attitude in dealing with others and in receiving the truth of God's word. Here we will learn some principles that will affect our daily interaction with others and will also lead us to receive the word of God in a way that will lead to the salvation of our souls.

James begins by addressing his audience by the term, *"My beloved brothers"*. What a warm and friendly greeting. The book is not just to brothers but is to *"beloved"* brothers. Think of the person that is most dear to you. Warm yourself with that knowledge and think of the depth of your love for that dear soul. Indescribable isn't it? That is the way we should love our brethren in Christ.

Peter said we should *"love one another earnestly from a pure heart,"* 1 Peter 1:22. Jesus commanded us to love each other just like He loved us, John 13:34-35. Being a child of God includes having a deep brotherly love that can only be described by the word *"beloved"*. Doesn't that sound like language that is usually reserved for one's mate or children? John wrote, *"Dear friends, since God so loved us, we also ought to love one another,"* 1 John 4:11. He, too, held his brethren in high esteem. Before we can achieve the teachings of James 1:19-21, we must achieve a deep love for God, for Jesus, and for each other.

I know what you are thinking. Some people are difficult to love. Yes that is true. However, isn't that also true in our own physical family? Yet we love our family members, warts and all. In the same way we must love each other just as Jesus loves us. Our church family needs to become our beloved brothers.

LEARNING THREE SERVANT QUALITIES

FIRST JEWEL: The quick ear. Sometimes we have trouble hearing spiritual things. As a matter of fact, sometimes we just don't listen to each other the way we should. That is why the Holy Spirit led James to instruct us to be quick to hear. Someone once said that God gave us two ears and one mouth for a reason – we should listen twice as much as we speak. I don't know where that came from, but it certainly makes good sense to me.

The Greek word for *"hear"* means *"to learn by hearing; to be informed, to listen."* It is very sad to read how the religious elite of Jesus' day rejected His words. They should have rejoiced in His coming. They should have been the very first to believe and obey His will. However, they were spiritually hard of hearing. In Matthew 13 Jesus taught many parables. He gave so many that it caused His disciples to ask Him why He was using so many of them. The Lord explained his actions by quoting Isaiah 6:9-10. Part of that passage says, *"You will indeed hear but never understand . . . For this people's heart has grown dull, and with their ears they can barely hear,"* Matthew 13:14-15.

We need to exercise our capacity to listen with nimble ears that are eager to learn. That is the sense of this passage. One might ask, *"What should we hear?"* What a good question. Here are a few passages that will help us answer that question. Romans 10:17 informs us that faith comes when we are quick to hear the words of Christ. One might say that the Holy Bible is our spiritual hearing aid. It gives us the ability to hear and to understand the spiritual truths God would have us to know.

In Matthew 7:24-26 we learn the need to hear with a view toward doing Jesus' words. If we don't obey our Savior when the storms of life appear our spiritual house will surely fall. Why else would Jesus say, *"Why do you call me Lord, Lord and not do what I tell you?"* Luke 6:46. Sometimes we stumble at His words because they are foreign to our personal practice or because they are different from what we were previously taught. Simply put, when we are quick to hear we will receive the words of God's truth with a mindset to do whatever He tells us to do.

SECOND JEWEL: The slow tongue. The Greek word *"slow"* is very interesting. It means *"slow, heavy, inactive in mind, stupid or slow to apprehend."* I remember a time when I came out of the dentist's office with a slow tongue. The medication to deaden my tooth also worked on my tongue. Until the medication wore off I talked rather like a tape recording going the wrong speed! I was literally s – l – o – w of speech.

The true reason for this command is to help us realize how important words can be. Read what Jesus said in Matthew 12:34-37. According to the Lord our own words will judge us in the last day. Oh, how careful we should be in what we say! Impulsive people have a difficult time with their tongue. They often put their tongue into action before putting their brain into gear.

Solomon wrote *"Even a fool who keeps silent is considered wise; when he closes his lips, he is deemed intelligent,"* Proverbs 17:28. Again, Solomon put it succinctly when he wrote, *"the tongue of the wise commends knowledge, but the mouth of the fool gushes folly,"* Proverbs 15:2. The slow tongue is not speaking of our literal speech patterns but is speaking of tempering our words with wisdom so that what comes out is good, acceptable and pleasing to God. *"Let your speech be seasoned with salt, so that you may know how you ought to answer each person,"* Colossians 4:6.

Do your best to think before you speak. Make a godly judgment to determine if the words you want to say are appropriate or even necessary for you to say. Your friends and associates will appreciate you for that trait. Strive to be slow to speak.

THIRD JEWEL: Controlling anger. Now we come to the problem of inappropriate anger. Sometimes people excuse unbridled anger as a bad personality trait. In so doing they relieve themselves of any personal responsibility for their behavior. They rationalize, *"I can't help it. I was born this way".* In and of itself anger is not a sin but it can certainly become such. That is why we are taught to be slow to anger. James 1:20 adds *"for the anger of man does not produce the righteousness that God requires".*

Study the meaning of the three Greek words translated by the English word *"anger"* that are described below. Anger is not necessarily a sin but it can certainly escalate to the point it becomes so. Controlling our anger is vital to our spiritual wellbeing.

Anger: *"Orgizomai"*: *"To be provoked to orge (anger); to be or become angry"*. Perhaps this is where anger begins. This word for anger is found in Ephesians 4:26, *"Be angry and do not sin, do not let the sun go down on your anger"*. Unless this type of anger is controlled it will lead us to sinful actions.

Anger: *"Thumos"*: The Greek word for anger in this passage means, *"the spirit that is breathed out . . . the working and fermenting of the mind, the demonstration of strong passion. 'Thumos' is the turbulent commotion of the mind, rage"*. How we deal with it will determine whether or not we sin. *"Know this, my beloved brothers: let every person be . . . slow to anger, for the anger of man does not produce the righteousness that God requires,"* James 1:19-20. The anger in verse 20 could easily escalate into sinful actions. Don't let your anger ferment so that it creates turbulent rage. Get rid of it as soon as possible.

Anger: *"Orge"*: is the word used in James 1:19, *"be slow to anger"*. This word means *"anger together with the desire for revenge. To kill, and all the tumults of passion which terminate in killing."* It is further defined, *"As it were, the heat of the fire. It is less sudden in its rise but more lasting. 'Orge' is the abiding settled habit of mind, the settled purpose of wrath.* This is anger that culminates in sin. This is the kind of anger that is vengeful and is very dangerous to our souls.

ANGER IS NOT ALWAYS A SIN

The Bible does not forbid us from becoming angry. It just warns us to do so slowly, and by all means, to control it. Anger becomes sin when we lose control and harbor ill will towards someone else. Unbridled anger will go beyond harboring ill will and will take revenge or some other harmful action against the person or object of our anger.

Look in your Bible concordance and read about the anger of God in the Old Testament. There are many occurrences of God's anger. Here are a few of those passages for your consideration. *"The LORD is slow to anger and abounding in steadfast love,"* Number 14:18. *"For they have rejected the law of the LORD of hosts, and have despised the word of the Holy one of Israel. Therefore the anger of the LORD was kindled against his people,"* Isaiah 5:24-25. *"But the people of Israel broke faith in regard to the devoted things . . . And the anger of the Lord burned against the people of Israel,* Joshua 7:1. God does get angry but He always does so in a righteous manner.

Jesus became angry too. Christ demonstrated His anger by turning over the tables of the moneychangers in the Temple, John 2:13-17. His righteous anger caused the people to say, *"Zeal for your house will consume me,"* John 2:17. Godly anger is not a sin.

DO NOT SIN IN YOUR ANGER
James 1:20
"For the anger of man does not produce the righteousness that God requires."

Ephesians 4:26 instructs us to be angry but not to sin. To accomplish this we must learn to be forgiving to those who have angered us. People who forgive each other before the sun goes down receive the benefit of not having to deal with excessive anger when they get up the next morning. The whole idea is for us to get over our anger quickly.

The reason we need to be slow to anger is clear. Our anger *"does not produce the righteousness God requires".* What a statement! It is vital for the Christian to control his anger if he hopes to live the kind of life God would have him to live. If you have an anger problem take it to God. With His help you can learn to overcome it. Unchecked anger makes it impossible to be truly righteous.

STEPS TOWARDS SALVATION
James 1:21
"Put away all filthiness and rampant wickedness and receive with meekness the implanted word, which is able to save your souls."

It is not enough just to have quick ears, a slow tongue and to be slow to anger. Before we are able to receive the word correctly we must put away all filthiness and rampant wickedness from our lives. Then we will be able to receive the implanted word of God that is able to save our soul. Don't you like the phrase *"implanted word"*? It means, *"Adapted for inward growth, to implant".* Sounds to me like having the word grow within us so that it actually becomes a part of who we are. The practice of putting God's word deeply in your heart will serve to help you go to a place called heaven. Below are two *"jewels"* found in James 1:21.

FIRST JEWEL: Put away your sins. We have already seen that James describes sin as filthiness and rampant wickedness. Does that seem like a strange way to speak to a believer in Christ? The truth is, we are not immune to sin just because we obeyed the Gospel of Christ. Paul warned the Galatian brethren that if they went back to their old way of life they would fall from grace, Galatians 5:4. It is possible for a child of God to sin in such a way that he falls from grace. Once they have fallen away they will be lost unless they repent and put away their sins.

Peter taught if a Christian went back to his former sinful practices after becoming a child of God his latter end would be worse than it was before he became a Christian, 2 Peter 2:20-22. He graphically described the status of a fallen Christian with these words: *"What the true proverb says has happened to them: 'The dog returns to its own vomit, and the sow, after washing herself, returns to wallow in the mire,'"* 2 Peter 2:22. Therefore, it is possible for a child of God to fall from his faithfulness and to be lost. These two examples serve to show us the need to be on guard lest we fall back into sinful practices and lose our reward. It seems very appropriate that James puts this verse immediately after his teaching on speaking, hearing, and anger.

SECOND JEWEL. Accept the word with meekness. The NIV uses the English word *"humbly"* while the ESV uses the word *"meekness"*. The Greek word used means *"mildness; the absence of any haughty self-sufficiency."* Meekness in this instance is the attitude we must have when we approach the word of God. We must accept what is written in the Bible because it contains the truth God revealed to man.

Many times I have attempted to teach people what the Bible has to say about salvation. Far too many times people have responded with the statement, *"I don't agree with what you just said"*. Unfortunately what was just said came directly from scripture. Scripture is not merely an opinion it is the word of the Lord. We will revisit the word meekness again in James 3:13. For now, let it suffice to say that without it our trust will not be in God but in our own abilities.

BE A DOER OF THE WORD!
James 1:22-25

"But be doers of the word, and not hearers only, deceiving yourselves. ²³For if anyone is a hearer of the word and not a doer, he is like a man who looks intently at his natural face in a mirror. ²⁴For he looks at himself and goes away and at once forgets what he was like. ²⁵But the one who looks into the perfect law, the law of liberty, and perseveres, being no hearer who forgets but a doer who acts, he will be blessed in his doing."

The emphasis now switches from hearing to doing. It is much easier to *"hear"* than to *"do"*. The word doer means, *"a poet; creative performance; a maker of anything."* It carries the idea of using our mind to creatively come up with ways to **DO** the things God would like for us to do. To do any less is to be deceived. The word translated *"deceive"* in this verse means *"to recon wrong; to cheat by false reasoning; to draw false conclusions"*. That is what happens to followers of Jesus who conclude they can be servants of the Lord without having to do anything.

Note: Up to this point we have studied two different Greek words that are translated by the English word *"deceive"*. These were found in James 1:16, and 1:22. Each word has a different shade of meaning. This illustrates the need to have a good Bible lexicon or dictionary so you can find the exact meaning of the original Greek word. Remember, an English dictionary will not help you discover the precise meaning of a Greek word.

Far too many people follow the lifestyle of the Israelites after they entered the Promised Land. Scripture tells us *"in those days there was no king in Israel. Everyone did what was right in his own eyes,"* Judges 21:25. False reckoning on their part led to a false sense of security. Is it any wonder Israel failed so miserably? They heard but they didn't do. How are we doing? Are we merely hearers of the word? Or, are we also doers?

FIRST JEWEL: Self-examination, James 2:23-24. Don't you love James' illustration of a person looking into a mirror and immediately forgetting what he looks like? For this person, life goes on as usual. There are few occasions when he actually becomes a doer of the word. This person forgets very easily and often he has no guilt feelings over his lack of performance.

Now we can really relate to a person looking into a mirror can't we! Have you ever walked through a shopping mall and passed by a full-length mirror only to be startled at how you look? Shocking isn't it? When one gets older such an experience becomes even more of a shock to the system!

Here I am, old, overweight, gray-headed, and looking a bit older in real life than I envision myself to be. The last time I saw myself in a shopping mall mirror I thought I was looking at someone else. Then, I realized I was looking at myself! *"Wow!"* I thought. *"I sure am getting old."* Like most people, when I left the mall I promptly forgot what I looked like and my life continued on as usual. However, every time I read James 1:22-24 I am reminded of the need to look more closely at my spiritual self. Doing so will help me grow spiritually.

The cure for forgetfulness is regular self-examination. Paul, the Apostle, wrote, *"I beat my body and make it my slave so that after I have preached to others, I myself will not be disqualified for the prize,"* 1 Corinthians 9:27. In 2 Corinthians 13:5, Paul gave good advice when he wrote, *"Examine yourselves to see whether you are in the faith; test yourselves. Do you not realize that Christ Jesus is in you – unless, of course, you fail the test?"* Strive with all your might to examine yourself honestly so that you will become both a hearer and a doer of the word. God will bless you when you do.

SECOND JEWEL: The perfect law of liberty, James 2:25. We now read of the person who *"looks into the perfect law, the law of liberty, and perseveres, being no hearer who forgets but a doer who acts, he will be blessed in his doing"*. The perfect law of liberty is another name for the Gospel of Christ. It is the message of the New Covenant, Hebrews 8:6-13. It is a perfect law – one that is better than the law given to Moses.

Since the perfect law of liberty speaks to the New Covenant we should spend a moment or two discussing what constitutes a covenant. A covenant is an agreement between two or more parties that places specific responsibilities on all concerned parties. While there were many covenants given in the Old Testament there are two major covenants that are of great significance. One was the Law given to Israel though Moses. This agreement was in effect from Mt. Sinai to the cross. (1446 B.C. to 29 A.D.) It contained the Law of Moses and was in effect until Jesus nailed it to His cross, Colossians 2:14-15. The Old Covenant has been fulfilled.

The New Covenant was given and ratified by Jesus Christ when He died on the cross. It is an everlasting covenant. The gospel, which is the message of the New Covenant, is to be taught throughout the entire world and is designed to bring sinful man into a covenant relationship with God. In the New Testament the word *"covenant"* often has the same meaning as a testament or will. A covenant is stronger than a promise because it puts obligations and requirements upon all parties of the agreement. It places conditions upon the participants.

Faithful adherence to the New Covenant will insure the salvation of our souls. In Hebrews 8:6-13 we learn how much greater the New Covenant is than the Law that was given through Moses. It is based upon better promises. One of the great blessings it contains is the knowledge that our sins have been forgiven and that God will remember them no more.

"But the one who looks into the perfect law, the law of liberty, and perseveres, being no hearer who forgets but a doer who acts, he will be blessed in his doing." The doer of the word goes to the perfect law of liberty to learn his part in keeping his covenant agreement with God. This person, in contrast to the forgetful hearer, makes every effort to be a faithful doer of the word. This person will be blessed for sure. That is because our great and wonderful God always blesses faithfulness!

ACCEPTABLE RELIGION
James 1:26-27

"If anyone thinks he is religious and does not bridle his tongue but deceives his heart, this person's religion is worthless. ²⁷Religion that is pure and undefiled before God, the Father, is this: to visit orphans and widows in their affliction and to keep oneself unstained from the world."

Are you a religious person? People often ask me the question, *"What is your religion?"* They want to know if I am Catholic, Protestant, Buddhist, or some other World Religion. Sadly, most people do not understand what the Bible means when it uses the word *"religion"*. How would you define it? Take a moment to consider your answer and then read on.

In the New Testament the Greek word translated *"religion"* means: *"religious observance, outward ceremonial service of religion."* Therefore, religion deals with rituals and observances we keep. Other people can clearly see what our religion is like by observing at the things we do when we come together to worship God.

For example, on the Lord's Day we come together to worship by singing, praying, taking the Lord's Supper, giving, and being taught the word of God. Those who observe our worship activities are provided with observable actions that help them see the nature of our religious activities.

Our religious service must conform to the instructions the Lord has given and we must do them from the heart. *"I will pray with my spirit, but I will also pray with my mind; I will sing with my spirit, but I will also sing with my mind,"* 1 Corinthians 14:15. To be acceptable to God our religious activities must be done from the heart and with proper understanding. Jesus said, *"God is spirit and those who worship him must worship in spirit and truth,"* John 4:24.

James deepens our understanding of the word religion by taking it out of the worship assembly and taking it into the world where we live. In James 1:26-27 we learn that true religion takes place when we control our tongue, when we are benevolent, and when we live a life that is unstained by the world.

PURE RELIGION

FIRST JEWEL: Religion requires tongue control, *"If anyone thinks he is religious and does not bridle his tongue but deceives his heart, this person's religion is worthless,"* James 1:26. A person who does not control his tongue deceives his own heart and his religion is worthless. The Greek word translated *"deceive"* is the same one used in James 1:22. It means, *"to recon wrong; to cheat by false reasoning; to draw false conclusions"*. The human tongue needs to be bridled like a horse so that we can control it. An unbridled tongue will produce deadly results. Read Matthew 12:34-37 once again to learn that we will be held accountable for every careless word we speak when we stand before the Lord on Judgment Day. We will come back to a discussion of the tongue when we study James 3:1-12.

SECOND JEWEL: Religion is benevolent. *"Religion that is pure and undefiled before God, the Father, is this: to visit orphans and widows in their affliction"*, James 1:27. Religion that is pure and undefiled before God actively helps those who are in need. This part of our religious activity is not practiced in a sanctuary on Sunday mornings. This is religion that goes out into the world to visit both widows and orphans in their affliction. To visit conveys the idea of supplying those things that are needed. A mere *"How are you today?"* is insufficient. We must provide for their needs. We will explore more on helping the needy when we study James 2:14-18.

When we speak of religion being benevolent it reminds me of Matthew 25:31-46. In this passage Jesus describes the judgment scene in a shocking manner. Those standing before the Lord on that day will not be judged by their faith and worship but by the acts of mercy they have done. Among those deeds were feeding the hungry, giving water to the thirsty, being hospitable to strangers, clothing the naked, visiting the sick and those in prison. This passage is similar in meaning to James 1:26-27.

Acceptable religion is not just about faith and worship. It is also about ministering to the needs of other people. *"As we have opportunity, let us do good to everyone, and especially to those who are of the household of faith,"* Galatians 6:10. When we serve those in need we are doing it to the Lord Himself. How will we stand on Judgment Day when it comes to visiting (helping) widows and orphans? If we don't help them how can we say our religion is *"pure and undefiled before God the Father?"* The answer is: we **CANNOT**!

THIRD JEWEL: Religion is holy, *"to keep oneself unstained from the world,"* James 1:27. Religion that is *"pure and undefiled before God"* requires personal purity. We must not be stained by the sinfulness that is so prevalent in this present world. God charged us to be *"holy for I am holy"*, 1 Peter 1:16. Our personal purity is first accomplished when we are washed in the blood of the Lamb. After that we must keep our lives pure by faithfully observing the teaching found in the word of God. Holiness is described in James 1:26 as keeping *"oneself unstained from the world"*. Such a quality is essential if we are to stand before the Lord as a person whose religion is to be well pleasing in God's sight.

"What religion are you?" someone asks. According to the criteria given by James there are several obvious traits that will define our religion beyond a doubt. The things important to him are not Sunday worship rituals. He lists the need for us to bridle (control) our tongue. Our religion will cause us to do deeds of benevolence for the widows and the orphans who are in need. We will live a life that is unstained from the sinful practices so prevalent in

the world in which we live. That is *"religion that is pure and undefiled before God, the Father"*.

DISCUSSION QUESTIONS:

1. Discuss the three servant qualities mentioned in James 1:19-21. Which one is most difficult for you? What steps can you take to strengthen your ability to display these qualities?

2. Talk about the different words translated by the English word anger.

3. Is anger ever justified? If so, when.

4. What two *"jewels"* will help us take steps towards salvation? Explain the difference between the steps mentioned.

5. Discuss James 1:23-24. How does looking into the mirror relate to the answer?

6. Discuss the perfect law of liberty. What is it?

7. Discuss the meaning of covenant.

8. Discuss the characteristics of true religion. Discuss ways we can do a better job of ministering to the needs of others.

Chapter 5

IMPARTIALITY TOWARDS ALL
James 2:1-13

James 2:1
"My brothers, show no partiality as you hold the faith of our Lord Jesus Christ, the Lord of glory."

THE SIN OF SHOWING PARTIALITY
I LIKE YOU BETTER!

James begins this section by telling us not to show partiality by discriminating among people from different segments of society. The specific case given is that of favoritism of the rich over the poor. In Romans 2:11 we learn that *"God shows no partiality"*. Since God treats all people without showing prejudice we must learn to do the same. As a child of God we must learn that any kind of discrimination based upon status in society, the color of one's skin, a person's nationality, their educational level, or any other basis that would lead us to think that some folks are *"better"* than others should not be practiced by the child of God.

Showing partiality does not mean we cannot have people in our lives that are very special. Even Jesus had His inner circle of Apostles (Peter, James and John). John seems to be the one called, *"the disciple whom Jesus loved,"* John 21:20; 24. Of course, that does not mean Jesus didn't love the other apostles.

Having someone who is very special to you is not the topic of James 2:1-13. The topic is discriminating by showing preferential treatment to a certain group of people in society while looking down upon others. What we must do is to love our neighbor as we love ourselves, Matthew 22:39. We are to love people even if they are poor and have little wealth or status in society. Jesus did a wonderful job of mixing with people from every segment of society.

I am humbled to know that God loves me just as much as He loves other human beings. The golden text of the Bible, John 3:16, shows the depth of His love for all people, *"For God so loved the world that He gave his only son"*. The Lord's love for all men is further expressed in 2 Peter 3:9 where we learn that Jehovah God is lovingly patient, *"not willing that any should perish, but that all should reach repentance"*. The Lord's universal love for all men proves that our Heavenly Father does not show partiality towards any living soul. We must love all people too. Make no mistake about it – showing partiality towards the rich or any other group of people is a sin, James 2:9.

I FOUND A FRIEND

When I was in High School I learned a valuable lesson about the evil of looking down on someone for no good reason. One day we had a substitute teacher come to our English class to fill in for our regular teacher. Our substitute was young and didn't know any of us. We could tell she didn't have much experience. When she called the roll none of us answered when our name was called. So our teacher began asking each of us the question, *"What is your name?"* The first student she asked gave the name of a popular movie star. Everyone laughed. That started a process where we all followed suit. When she asked me my name, I said *"Roy Rogers"*. I guess that dates me a bit, but at that time he was the *"King of the Cowboys"*.

Just as our teacher was reaching a zenith of frustration a new student walked into the room. He was sent to our English class after his enrollment was completed. The teacher asked him his name and he said *"Gene Autrey"*. The classroom roared with laughter. Of course he was not the *"Singing Cowboy"* who later owned the Los Angeles Angels baseball team. He only shared the same name.

Our poor teacher could stand no more so she yelled at him at the top of her lungs and ordered him out of the room. Gene returned in a few minutes with the school Principal by his side. This seasoned administrator quickly saw what had been going on in our room. He calmly introduced our new student, Gene Autrey, to the class. Had we not been tormenting our substitute teacher, Gene would not have had such a traumatic introduction to Tucumcari High School.

Of course the story spread throughout the school and as a result many of my classmates gave Gene a difficult time. They didn't take the time to learn what a nice person he was. I made the decision to befriend him. In a very short time Gene and I became dear friends. Even after all these years, he is a friend of mine. We communicate with each other from time to time. My English class was guilty of judging Gene by the circumstances of the day and by the name he wore. It turned into a huge blessing for me that I didn't follow suit. Showing partiality, prejudice, or preferential treatment is not something a child of God should do.

A LOOK AT BOTH RICH AND POOR
James 2:1-3

"My brothers, show no partiality as you hold the faith in our Lord Jesus Christ, the Lord of glory. ² For if a man wearing a gold ring and fine clothing comes into your assembly, and a poor man in shabby clothing also comes in, ³ and if you pay attention to the one who wears the fine clothing and say, "You sit here in a good place," while you say to the poor man, "You stand over there," or, "Sit down at my feet."

As you read through the text it appears that the rich people in question were not even Christians. That is indicated in James 2:6 where we learn that the rich oppressed the church members by dragging them into courts of law. They also blasphemed the name by which they were called. Isn't it strange that a group of people who were openly mistreating Christians were being shown preferential treatment when they met together in their assembly?

The word *"assembly"* is from the Greek word meaning *"Synagogue"*. The fact that the Synagogue is mentioned in this verse gives us additional evidence for accepting an early date for this epistle. Early Christians often met in the Synagogue to teach the Jews about Jesus the Messiah. Read Acts 6:8-9; 13:13-16; 17:1-3 for a sampling of this truth. The rich who were coming to the Synagogue were being favored by the Christians simply because they were rich not because they were such a loveable people.

It is not unusual for the rich to expect special treatment. After all, they are people of means and they feel like they deserve to be treated in a way that shows them honor. The Christians in the assembly said to the rich, *"You sit here in a good place"*. This favoritism was shown because of the gold rings and fine clothing being worn by the rich. It was also shown because of their status in society.

Read Luke 14:7-11, the parable of the wedding feast, to learn about the practice of giving seats of honor to *"special"* people. In this parable Jesus warned against choosing to sit too close to the head of the table (a place reserved for honored guests) lest someone more important than you were to arrive and you be requested to move to a lower seat. While this custom does not necessarily indicate the sin of showing preferential treatment it certainly could lend itself towards such a practice.

Jesus suggested sitting at the lowest seat (showing humility) so the host would say, *"friend, move up higher"*. In this way, you would be honored instead of embarrassed. The truth is, it is not important where we sit but, rather, whom we serve and how we treat other people.

THE POOR

The poor men in James 2:3 were dressed in shabby clothing. When they arrived at the Synagogue they were paid little attention or, perhaps were ignored altogether. Some of the poor were acknowledged in the following way. *"You stand over there,"* or, *"Sit down at my feet"*.

How would you feel if a poorly dressed person came into your worship assembly? Suppose a *"street person"* came into the assembly shabbily dressed and not too clean. Suppose he sat down right beside you. How would you feel about that? Would you be tempted to say, *"You stand over there!"* What would Jesus do? He might say, *"Today I will eat at your house."* We must hold faith in our Lord Jesus Christ without showing partiality.

MAKING A CASE AGAINST PARTIALITY, James 2:1-11.

FIRST JEWEL: Partiality is not consistent with Christ's glory, *"My brothers, show no partiality as you hold the faith in our Lord Jesus Christ, the Lord of glory,"* James 2:1.

We are a people who hold faith in Jesus Christ as the Lord of glory. How dare we show partiality to the rich or to anyone else on this planet! I love the fact that Jesus spent time with all segments of society. He did not treat the poor and downtrodden in a prejudicial way nor did He put the rich on a pedestal. Jesus spent time with tax collectors and sinners, Luke 19:1-10. The Lord went with the tax collector, Zacchaeus, because He was interested in saving his soul.

From Luke 19:10 we learn that seeking and saving the lost was the reason Jesus came to this earth. We should follow the Lord's example by showing honor to all men regardless of whether they are rich or poor.

SECOND JEWEL: Partiality is based on outward appearance, *"For if a man wearing a gold ring and fine clothing comes into your assembly, and a poor man in shabby clothing also comes in, ³ and if you pay attention to the one who wears the fine clothing and say, "You sit here in a good place," while you say to the poor man, 'You stand over there,' or, "Sit down at my feet,"* James 2:2-3.

These believers were treating the rich with preferential treatment because they wore gold rings and fine clothing. At the same time, they treated the poor with prejudice because they wore shabby clothes. They were judging a person based upon how he looked.

Long ago God sent the prophet Samuel to choose a King to replace Saul. He went to Bethlehem to the house of Jesse to anoint one of his sons to be the next King of Israel. Eliab was the first to come before the prophet. Samuel thought *"Surely the LORD'S anointed is before me,"* 1 Samuel 16:6. God told Samuel not to look on outward appearances *"for the Lord sees not as man sees: man looks on the outward appearance, but the LORD looks on the heart,* 1 Samuel 16:7. This process continued until seven of Jesse's sons had passed before the prophet.

None of the first seven men was the one God had chosen to replace King Saul so Samuel asked if there were any other sons. There was one more, a lad named David. He was keeping the sheep while the other sons stood before the prophet. David was described as being *"ruddy and had beautiful eyes and was handsome,"* 1 Samuel 16:12. When David entered the presence of Samuel God revealed the news, *"This is the one".* Shortly thereafter David was anointed to be the next King of Israel!

Aren't you glad God looks at the inner man, where a person's true beauty dwells, instead of looking at outward appearances? Showing partiality makes us judges with evil thoughts. Who knows the heart of a man except God Himself? We can make some judgments based on what a person does but we must be sure we do not base our opinion strictly upon how someone looks.

THIRD JEWEL: Partiality is not the way of God, *"Have you not then made distinctions among yourselves and become judges with evil thoughts? ⁵ Listen, my beloved brothers, has not God chosen those who are poor in the world to be rich in faith and heirs of the kingdom, which he has promised to those who love him? ⁶ But you have dishonored the poor man. Are not the rich the ones who oppress you, and the ones who drag you into court? ⁷ Are they not the ones who blaspheme the honorable name by which you were called?"* James 2:4-7.

The Christians to whom James wrote chose the rich over the poor making distinctions between the two groups. James instructs us that God chose the poor who are rich in faith to be heirs of the kingdom. The key to being acceptable in God's sight is to be rich in faith. Perhaps poor people realize their need for divine help more readily than wealthy people. Of necessity the poor look to the Lord for help.

The church in Laodicea had many who were blessed with great riches. They were proud of their achievements. However, they were condemned as being *"wretched, pitiable, poor, blind, and naked"*, Revelation 3:17. God's promises are made to those who are rich in faith. They will become heirs of the kingdom of God. This is true regardless of whether a person is rich or poor.

Finally, the rich were oppressing the very ones who were honoring them. They drug the believers into court in order to sue them. They blasphemed the honorable name by which the believers were called. This name could have been disciple of Christ, Christian, or child of God. The rich who were being shown preferential treatment were guilty of persecuting the very Christians who were honoring them! Shocking isn't it? Showing partiality is not the way of God.

FOURTH JEWEL: Showing Partiality Brings Judgment Against The Sinner, *"If you really fulfill the royal law according to the Scripture, 'You shall* *love your neighbor as yourself,' you are doing well. ⁹ But if you show partiality, you are committing sin and are convicted by the law as transgressors. ¹⁰ For whoever keeps the whole law but fails in one point has become accountable for all of it. ¹¹ For he who said, 'Do not commit adultery,' also said, 'Do not murder.' If you do not commit adultery but do murder, you have become a transgressor of the law,"* James 2:8-11. The Royal Law is defined in this text as the commandment *"to love your neighbor as yourself"*. According to 1 John 4:20-21, it is impossible to love God whom we have not seen and hate our brother whom we have seen. The consequence of breaking the Royal Law is sin. James 2:8-9 explains what sin we commit when we show partiality. The sin is to break the commandment to love our neighbor as ourselves, the Royal Law.

To break even one point in the law is to become accountable to the entire law. If you don't commit adultery but do commit murder you have become a transgressor of the law. This illustration is given to show us the severity of the sin of showing partiality. Does it amaze you to learn that the Holy Spirit uses the illustration of murder to explain to us the sin of showing partiality?

James has made a biblical case against showing partiality. The lost world in which we live needs those of us who are Christians to lead the way in treating all men without prejudice or partiality. It does not matter if a person is rich or poor, black or white, or if they are a different nationality than us. If we love our neighbor as our self we will take the opportunity to teach them about the Lord Christ Jesus. Once saved, they will become our beloved brethren in Christ. The Lord will bless us when we treat all people with the honor and respect that is due them.

THE BASIS FOR JUDGMENT IS MERCY
James 2:12-13

"So speak and so act as those who are to be judged under the law of liberty. ¹³ For judgment is without mercy to one who has shown no mercy. Mercy triumphs over judgment."

THE LAW OF LIBERTY

James concludes his discussion on partiality by mentioning the law of liberty and the need to be merciful. What is the law of liberty? There are at least two interpretations to its meaning.

Some authorities believe it means entire gospel message. They explain that when one obeys the law of the Gospel he is made free from sin. Therefore the gospel is the law of liberty. However, is that what the Holy Spirit had in mind in this passage?

Others believe the law of liberty refers to mercy. This interpretation is based on the very next verse, which tells us, *"For judgment is without mercy to one who has shown no mercy. Mercy triumphs over judgment."* This explanation makes more sense to this author than the first explanation. If we keep the law of liberty, by showing mercy to others, it is highly unlikely we will commit the sin of showing partiality.

MERCY TRIUMPHS OVER JUDGMENT

The second idea shared in these verses is the need to show mercy to others. To be judged only on the basis of law means condemnation for everyone. For that reason, James said, *"mercy triumphs over judgment".* That is good news because to be judged strictly according to the law is to be condemned. However, mercy from God will only be extended to those who show mercy to others.

Mercy means *"a feeling of sympathy, active compassion, the desire of relieving the miserable".* The Christians to whom James wrote gave preferential treatment to the rich but showed no mercy to the poor. Therefore they would receive no mercy from God. Reflection on this truth should help us to treat others with much more mercy. *"Blessed are the merciful for they shall receive mercy,"* Matthew 5:7.

In the parable of the unforgiving servant, Matthew 18:21-35, Jesus illustrated the truth that mercy is conditional. In this parable a servant owed a sum of money beyond his ability to pay. The debtor pleaded with his Master for more time so he could pay the debt. It was a huge debt of 10,000 talents. One talent equaled 20 years wages. This meant he owed his master 200,000 years worth of wages! How could anyone pay a debt that large? He begged his Master for time and was granted mercy instead. He was forgiven the entire debt. Sounds a little like what Jesus did for us on the cross doesn't it?

This fortunate servant went out and found a man who owed him one hundred denarii, about 100 days wages, and demanded payment. When the man could not pay, he put him into debtors prison until he paid all that he owed. Isn't it strange how we can receive mercy from God, or from someone else, and then be so spiritually blind that we fail to repay someone else with the same act of mercy we, ourselves, recently received?

When the Master heard about the action of this mean and unforgiving servant he rescinded his mercy and put the ungrateful servant into prison until he paid the debt he owed. Of course that meant a life sentence. The debt was far too great for him to ever repay. The lesson is simple. We must show mercy to others if we expect to receive any from the Lord. In our prejudicial world, it would be wise for all of us to learn to be more accepting towards those who are different from us. A large dose of mercy will help us to conquer prejudice. We must guard against showing preferential treatment to some people while looking down upon others. We must treat people fairly because to do any less is a sin.

DISCUSSION QUESTIONS:

1. Discuss the problem of prejudice and showing partiality. Have you ever experienced it yourself?

2. Is showing partiality an *"American"* problem or is it a worldwide issue?

3. Discuss the following *"jewels"* that make a case against showing partiality.

    a. Partiality is not consistent with Christ's glory.

    b. Partiality is based on outward appearance.

    c. Partiality is not the way of God.

    d. Showing partiality brings judgment against the sinner.

4. Discuss God's mercy. What does it mean? How can we show mercy to one another?

Chapter 6

RELATIONSHIP OF FAITH AND WORKS
James 2:14-26

James 2:14

"What good is it, my brothers, if someone says he has faith but does not have works? Can that faith save him?"

PRELIMINARY CONSIDERATIONS

We now turn our thoughts to how faith affected the life and practice of believers in the First Century. This chapter will contrast the words *"faith"* and *"works"* to see how they interact. In addition to defining the two words we will look at how James uses them and contrast them to the usage of the Apostle Paul. This is necessary due to a misunderstanding by many scholars and Bible teachers who believe there is a conflict between James and Paul. I am convinced there is no contradiction at all. Rather, the two authors are looking at works from two different perspectives.

First, let's define the word *"works"*. The Greek word is defined as *"work, deed, the result or object of employment . . . that which is brought into being or accomplished by labor, the thing wrought"*. Simply put, work is that which occupies our time and effort.

The word *"faith"* comes from a Greek word that is translated by three English words, **faith**, **believe**, and **belief**. The lexicon definition is *"firm persuasion, the conviction which is based upon hearing, not upon sight, or knowledge, a firmly relying confidence in what we hear from God in His word."* When reading your Bible please remember that all three words have the same meaning. It is important to realize how important faith in God is to all of us. *"Without faith it is impossible to please him,"* Hebrews 11:6. The source of our faith is the word of God, Romans 10:17.

WHAT FAITH LOOKS LIKE

The Bible, itself, shows us what Biblical faith looks like. Below are three facets of faith found in scripture. Looking at the Biblical usage of a word often helps us gain a deeper understanding of its meaning. It is always a good idea to look in a Lexicon or Bible Dictionary to discover a word's meaning but it is also vital to see how the word is used in the word of God. Doing so will help us grasp the subtly of meaning suggested by its usage.

FIRST JEWEL: Mental Belief. *"Faith is the assurance of things hoped for the conviction of things not seen"*, Hebrews 11:1. This is the first biblical explanation of faith we want to discover. It is the part of faith that believes based on the testimony of the Bible. No man has seen God but we believe that He is. The prophet Daniel put it this way, *"there is a God in heaven,"* Daniel 2:28. Daniel's faith was likely based upon convictions brought about by observations from nature, Psalm 19:1-2, by the words of the Bible, and by God's dealings with the Israelites over the centuries.

We have not seen the resurrected Lord but we believe He literally rose from the grave and proved Himself to be alive after His crucifixion during a time span of 40 days, Acts 1:3. The testimony of the Apostles concerning the resurrected Lord produces faith. Read 1 Corinthians 15:1-58 to gain some excellent information on the importance of the resurrection of Jesus to those of us who believe.

Our faith is based upon the reliability of the Scriptures. The bible provides reliable evidence that is not based on manmade fables and myths. Faith is not merely grasping at straws. Jesus pronounced a blessing upon those who believed that He rose from the dead even though they were not privileged to see Him in person, John 20:29. This is the part of faith I call **mental belief.**

SECOND JEWEL: Wholehearted trust. Abraham was *"fully convinced that God was able to do what he had promised,"* Romans 4:21. This passage refers to the promise God made to him that he would become the father of many Nations, Genesis 12:1-3. This promise was made before Abraham even had a son. When a person believes in God he puts his full weight upon His promises.

Even after twenty-five years had passed Abraham still had total confidence that the promise to give him a son would be fulfilled. Abraham believed God even though he was old and his wife was past the age of childbearing. To be a person of faith a person must wholeheartedly trust that God means what he says. Read Romans 4:13-25 for more details.

In times past God spoke to men through the prophets and sometimes through angels. Today, the Lord speaks to us through the Holy Bible. In the Old Testament we read the phrase *"thus says the Lord"* thousands of times. Those inspired words were written down so we could know our Heavenly Father and His commandments. As history unfolded it became crystal clear to men of God that the Lord does keep His promises. Men of faith became more and more confident as history unfolded because they were able to see so many of the promises of God being fulfilled.

In the New Testament we learn that the men who wrote the Bible were *"carried along by the Holy Spirit,"* 2 Peter 1:21. Therefore their message was not the words of man but the words of Almighty God. This is the process called the inspiration of the Bible. *"All scripture is breathed out by God,"* 2 Timothy 3:16. The phrase *"breathed out"* is translated by the word *"inspired"* by many translations of the Bible. To have faith is to be fully convinced that what we hear from God in His word is true. This is the part of faith I call **wholehearted trust**.

THIRD JEWEL: Active obedience. Hebrews chapter eleven is full of people of faith who did exactly what God asked them to do. By faith Abel offered a more acceptable sacrifice than Cain, Hebrews 11:4. By faith Noah built an ark to the saving of his household, Hebrews 11:7. By faith Abraham offered up Isaac believing God would raise his son from the dead, Hebrews 11:17-19. The list of faithful servants in Hebrews is long. Read this glorious chapter to see what each hero of the faith did in response to God's commandments. Faith is not obedience. However, obedience is the natural by-product of true faith. Biblical faith always does something.

In James 2:14 the following question is asked, *"What good is it, my brothers, if someone says he has faith but does not have works? Can that faith save him?"* The answer is a resounding **NO!** If you understand the Biblical explanation of faith (which is **Mental Acceptance**, **Wholehearted Trust**, and **Active Obedience**) you will seek ways to serve the living God. This type of faith exhibits what I call **active obedience**.

COMPARING JAMES TO PAUL

Some scholars find a conflict between James and Paul. Some noted theologians, including Martin Luther, even go so far as to suggest that the book of James should be excluded from the New Testament altogether. In my view, James definitely belongs to the canon of Scripture. The scholars who find a conflict between the teaching of James and Paul do not understand the harmony that existed between these two men of God. They think James taught we must work in order to be saved while Paul taught that we are saved by grace *"not a result of works, so that no one may boast,"* Ephesians 2:9. At first glance this does sound contradictory doesn't it? If James did teach that a person must work in order to be saved then he was in error. What do you think?

Do contradictions really exist? Consider the following. Paul spoke of the fallacy of doing works of the law as a means of achieving salvation. James spoke of works as the natural expression of faith. Paul lets us know that works of the law can do nothing to earn us our salvation. James speaks of works as something a bondservant would do as he served his Master. These two men were looking at works from different perspectives.

PAUL'S TEACHING

Works of the law do not save us. Read what Paul wrote, *"For by works of the law no human being will be justified in his sight, since through the law comes knowledge of sin,"* Romans 3:20. From this passage we learn than a person cannot work his way into heaven. The Apostle is approaching works from the standpoint of earning salvation through law keeping. That is not how salvation comes to mankind. We are saved by faith and not by works of the Law, Ephesians 2:8-10. The purpose of the law is to provide us with knowledge of sin. The law was given because of sin, Galatians 3:19. Jesus came to take away sin.

God is not in our debt. Paul commended Abraham's faith as the basis of his righteousness. It was not granted on the basis of his works. *"For if Abraham was justified by works, he has something to boast about, but not before God. For what does the Scripture say? 'Abraham believed God, and it was counted to him as righteousness,'"* Romans 4:2-3. As just stated by Paul, if coming to God and becoming righteous were based on works, then Abraham had something to boast about. However, Abraham *"believed God, and it was counted to him as righteousness"*. Works of the Law do not justify us in God's sight. We are justified by our faith, Romans 5:1.

Both of these passages point out that we are saved by our faith and not by works of the law. The law only brings us knowledge of sin. Paul is teaching the fallacy of works as a means for achieving salvation. Clearly works of the law cannot earn our salvation. Jesus explained the position works takes in the life of a bondservant when He said, *"When you have done all that you were commanded, say 'We are unworthy servants, we have only done what was our duty,'"* Luke 17:10. You might want to read Luke 17:7-10 to get the whole picture.

Saved by grace not by works. Read Ephesians 2:8-10 for a deeper look at the correlation between grace and works. In this passage Paul clearly states we are saved by grace through faith. He presents salvation as a gift from God. He also points out that salvation is not of works lest we boast. Salvation is God's work. Salvation comes by His grace through faith not by any works that we do.

Immediately after telling us that our salvation is given to us by God's grace, Paul tells us of our need to work. *"For we are his workmanship, created in Christ Jesus, for good works, which God prepared beforehand, that we should walk in them"*, Ephesians 2:10. At first glance it looks like Paul contradicts himself, but he doesn't. We come to God in faith, and we are saved by the blood of Jesus Christ our Lord. God saves us by grace, through faith. Nothing we have done, no work we have accomplished, earns us our salvation. We are blood bought and can never say God is our debtor. If works saved us we would have every right to boast of our accomplishments.

Serving the Lord is one of the reasons God made man. Paul understood and practiced this truth. He wrote, *"By the grace of God I am what I am, and his grace toward me was not in vain. On the contrary, I worked harder than any of them, though it was not I, but the grace of God that is with me,"* 1 Corinthians 15:10. Paul believed that those who are saved naturally give themselves in service to the Master. Such service can be described by the word *"work"*. So, we conclude that Paul agrees with James when he speaks of those who are saved by grace. Once we are saved we gladly work in service to the Lord.

JAMES' TEACHING

In James 2:14-26, James presents works from the standpoint of the service rendered by the saved. We could call that obedient faith. Our next chapter, entitled **"Faith Without Works Is Dead"**, will develop the teaching of James 2:14-26 more fully.

For now, please read the following passages from the book of James. They speak loudly of the need for people of faith to work.

"What good is it, my brothers, if someone says he has faith but does not have works? Can that faith save him?" James 2:14. Implied answer: **No it cannot!** In our explanation of faith, we learned that true faith produces active obedience.

"Faith by itself, if it does not have works, is dead," James 2:17. When we do not serve the Lord by doing good works in His name we are dead. Sounds like a sin to me. After all, Paul wrote, *"The wages of sin is death,"* Romans 6:23.

"Do you want to be shown, you foolish person, that faith apart from works is useless?" James 2:20. In this passage we learn that anyone who separates faith from works is a foolish person. The person saved by grace will gratefully work for the furtherance of the kingdom of God.

"You see that a person is justified by works and not by faith alone," James 2:24. Here we learn that faith plus works equals justification. You just cannot have Biblical faith without works.

"For as the body apart from the spirit is dead, so also faith apart from works is dead," James 2:26. This is a strong argument for faith plus works. Human life depends upon the body and the spirit being vibrantly joined to each other. If the spirit departs from the body the person dies. The same is true for faith and works. There can be no life apart from works.

JAMES AND PAUL DO AGREE

The Apostle Paul's work was to preach the gospel. He did not preach in order to receive credit to his account. He spoke out of necessity. *"For if I preach the gospel, that gives me no ground for boasting for necessity is laid upon me. Woe to me if I do not preach the gospel!"* 1 Corinthians 9:16. Once he was saved by the grace of God, Paul's faith issued in works.

As stated earlier in this chapter, James and Paul approached faith and works from two different perspectives. Paul spoke of the fallacy of doing works of the law as a means of achieving salvation. James spoke of works as the natural expression of faith. There is no conflict between the two.

GOD GAVE MAN WORK TO DO

Some people misunderstand the fact that God has always expected man to work. In the Garden of Eden man was given the charge to keep the garden, Genesis 2:15. If we were required to do physical work why would we think we have no spiritual work to do? The Almighty gave mankind two kinds of work to do during their lifetime. He gave us physical and spiritual work to do.

FIRST JEWEL: Physical labor. We must work to supply for our physical needs. We just noticed that God put Adam in the Garden of Eden to work in the garden. After the fall of Adam and Eve man's work became more difficult. Now the ground was cursed to bring forth thorns and thistles. After his sin, Adam would have to work by the sweat of his brow, Genesis 3:17-19. However, there has never been a free ride. Man has always been expected to work.

Even though the Apostle Paul had the right to be fed by the brethren he did not do so. Instead he worked with his own hands to supply for his needs. He concluded by saying, *"If anyone is not willing to work, let him not eat,"* 2 Thessalonians 3:7-10. The Bible disapproves of the lazy person. *"Slothfulness casts into a deep sleep and an idle person will suffer hunger,"* Proverbs 19:15. Because of the necessity to work, God sends ample blessings upon all men, both good and evil, so they can receive the basic necessities of life.

Solomon also wrote, *"The sluggard says, 'there is a lion in the road! There is a lion in the streets!' As a door turns on its hinges, so does a sluggard on his bed. The sluggard buries his hand in the dish; it wears him out to bring it back to his mouth,"* Proverbs 26:13-16. This lazy man invents reasons not to go out and work for a living. His love for sleep is likened unto a door swinging on a hinge! He just cannot bring himself to get up and work for a living. Even eating becomes a chore for this slothful man. He is so lazy it wears him out to bring his hand back from the dish with food on it!

GOD'S LOVING CARE

We all realize there are many legitimate reasons why a person cannot work. Many people do not work because of poor health. A poor economy sometimes makes it very difficult for people to find work. I'm sure there are other reasons why a person cannot work. However, under normal circumstances, people are expected to work in order to supply for the necessities of life.

Jesus knew people were concerned about having food and proper clothing. In the Sermon on the Mount, Matthew 6:25-34, we find a long discussion on this topic. Read it to be reminded that God understands our need for food and clothing. Jesus taught we should not be overly concerned over receiving the bare necessities of life because God, Himself, knows that we need them.

If God cares for the plants and the birds, then He will certainly supply us with what we need to sustain life. Jesus promised we would receive our basic needs if we sought first, *"the kingdom of God and his righteousness"*. By doing so, *"all these things* (the necessities of life) *will be added to you,"* Matthew 6:33.

SECOND JEWEL: Spiritual labor. The word of God teaches, *"Whatever you do, in word or deed, do everything in the name of the Lord Jesus, giving thanks to God the Father through him,"* Colossians 3:17. What a beautiful passage to demonstrate the need for us to become engaged in spiritual labor. This is work we accomplish in the name of the Lord.

In this chapter we are looking at faith and works. We are exploring many ideas that are not found in the book of James. Yet, they are important truths for us to study before we begin our discussion of James 2:14-26.

The ideas that follow illustrate spiritual labor with five examples designed to help us to remain productive servants of God. Study them carefully in order to gain more understanding of our personal responsibility to be actively engaged in serving the Lord.

We are vines, John 15:1-8. Of course, Jesus is the branch and God is the vinedresser. As grapevines we are expected to bear grapes. I can't imagine a grapevine being allowed to stay on the branch if it only produced a single grape. Can you? In this example, Jesus taught that barren vines would be cut off and cast into the fire. As grapevines, we are to bear much fruit, because this is what the Lord intended for us to do. In this way God will be glorified, John 15:8.

We are olive branches, Romans 11:17-24. God cut off unfaithful Israel and grafted the Gentile Christians into His Olive tree. The original tree depicted faithful Israel. Because they became unfruitful they were cut off and the faithful Gentile Christians were cut from a wild olive tree and grafted into the tree of God. We read that if the Jews repented and obeyed the gospel they would be grafted back into the fruitful tree. In order to remain a part of God's olive tree fruitfulness is required by all the branches. Otherwise, whether a Jew or a Gentile, they would be cut off and would experience the severity of God.

We are Christian soldiers, 2 Timothy 2:3-4. *"Share in suffering as a good solder of Christ Jesus. No soldier gets entangled in civilian pursuits since his aim is to please the one who enlisted him."* A soldier must be totally dedicated to his task. He must concentrate on battlefield requirements. Who would say that a soldier doesn't work? They have a very difficult job to do. We must be good Christian soldiers. You might want to read Ephesians 6:10-17 to be reminded about the armor to be worn by the Christian soldier.

We are athletes, 2 Timothy 2:5. *"An athlete is not crowned unless he competes according to the rules."* We all know that athletic proficiency requires much diligent work. In addition an athlete must follow the rules of his race, otherwise he will be disqualified. Suppose a runner ran the quarter mile race in the fastest time in the history of the world. However, suppose he ran in the wrong direction. Would he be crowned? Since he ran the wrong way he broke the rules. As a result he would not receive the victor's crown. Since this is true of an athlete in a sporting event how much more will it be true of the Christian *"athlete"!*

We are farmers, 2 Timothy 2:6. *"It is the hardworking farmer who ought to have the first share of the crops."* In this verse, the farmer is described as being *"hardworking"*. Have you ever been around a successful farmer? If so, you know how diligent and hardworking he must be. In like manner the *"Christian farmer"* needs to labor for the Master. When he does, he will be blessed to receive the first fruits of his labor. For certain, there is nothing as gratifying as seeing your spiritual labor bring forth fruit.

This chapter has been dedicated to proving that James and Paul do not contradict each other on the topic of works. Faithful people always work diligently to do the things that bring glory to God. A great many of God's faithful prophets and Apostles excelled in their labors far above the abilities of ordinary men. They left us a challenging example to follow in their steps. We will close with the words of 1 Corinthians 15:10-11.

"But by the grace of God I am what I am, and his grace toward me was not in vain. On the contrary, I worked harder than any of them, though it was not I, but the grace of God that is with me. Whether then it was I or they, so we preach and so you believed."

DISCUSSION QUESTIONS:

1. Define the words *"work"* and *"faith"*.

2. Discuss the three "jewels" showing us what faith looks like in the Bible.

3. Discuss the difference in perspective between James and Paul's teaching on works.

4. Explain how Ephesians 2:8-10 uses the idea of works in verses 8-9 and again in verse 10. Explain why they are not contradictory.

5. Discuss Adam and the rest of mankind's need to work. Is working God's punishment to sinful man or is it something else?

6. Give some examples of the spiritual work we have been given to do. You may find help for this in Galatians 5:22-24 and Romans 12:3-8.

Chapter 7

FAITH WITHOUT WORKS IS DEAD
James 2:14-26

James 2:14
"What good is it, my brothers, if someone says he has faith but does not have works? Can that faith save him?"

SAVING FAITH ILLUSTRATED

Now we turn to some practical illustrations of saving faith that issues in works. We should carefully put these teachings into practice as we walk in the steps of Jesus as God's dear children. We begin with two rhetorical questions. *"What good is it, my brothers, if someone says he has faith but does not have works? Can that faith save him?"*

This type of questioning implies there is only one correct answer. That answer is faith must be coupled with works if it is to have any value. The second question, *"Can faith save him?"* requires a negative answer. That is because faith alone (apart from works) is not saving faith. The remainder of the chapter provides irrefutable evidence that answers both of the questions asked in James 2:14.

The scripture that follows naturally divides itself into four sections. They are: **HELPING THE NEEDY**, 2:15-18, **DEMONS BELIEVE AND SHUDDER**, 2:19-20, **THE EXAMPLE OF ABRAHAM**, 2:21-24, and **THE EXAMPLE OF RAHAB**, 2:25-26. These points will be discussed in more detail in the pages that follow.

HELPING THE NEEDY
James 2:15-18
"If a brother or sister is poorly clothed and lacking in daily food,

> *^{16} and one of you says to them, 'Go in peace, be warmed and filled,' without giving them the things needed for the body, what good is that? ^{17} So also faith by itself, if it does not have works, is dead. ^{18} But someone will say, 'You have faith and I have works.' Show me your faith apart from your works, and I will show you my faith by my works."*

How do you help a brother or sister who is poorly clothed and lacking in daily food? Are mere words sufficient or do we need to provide them with more than our words of encouragement? It seems to me the needy would think we were out of our minds if all we did for them was say, *"Go in peace, be warmed and filled"*. All too often I have seen people look with distain upon people in need and offer remarks such as, *"If that person would just go to work they wouldn't have to come begging to us!"* Such remarks are callous and do not consider the circumstances that put the poor and hungry brother in a situation where they needed our help. When we say the right words to the needy but do not give them what they need, *"what good is that?"* James 2:16.

Jesus taught us to pray to God asking Him to *"give us this day our daily bread,"* Matthew 6:11. This wonderful verse encourages us to ask God to provide our sustenance. However, there are times when good people need the help of their brothers in Christ in order to make it through difficult times. As poor as He was, Jesus had a fund from which He provided assistance to the poor. Judas carried Jesus' moneybag and was supposed to use part of it to help those in need. See John 12:4-6.

Isn't it interesting to learn that one of the problems of the early church was a failure to give some of the Christian widows their daily distribution of goods, Acts 6:1-7? I am convinced that the church of today does not take the charge to help those in need as seriously as our brethren who lived in the First Century. There may be some benevolent churches that assist widows on a daily basis but I don't know where they are. How tolerant would you be if such a need arose in your congregation? Would you want to help the widows or would you say, *"I think it's about time these people helped themselves!"*

Perhaps the problem is too many scam artists have burned us by giving false claims about their needs and wasting our benevolence funds. However, we must find a way to help those who are truly in need of our help. We have a God given responsibility to help those among us who are poor. We also need to assist people in the community who are not Christians who lack the basic necessities of life. *"So, then, as we have opportunity, let us do good to everyone, and especially to those who are of the household of faith,"* Galatians 6:10. This is not an easy task for us to accomplish but it is something that needs to be addressed by those of us who believe.

FIRST JEWEL: The early church helped its own. In the First Century, many churches took up special collections at the urging of the Apostle Paul. Benevolence funding was collected over a long period of time. At the end of his third missionary journey the Apostle Paul laid the money at the feet of the elders in Jerusalem. Paul told Festus, *"Now after several years I came to bring alms to my nation and to present offerings,"* Acts 24:17.

Read about this huge joint effort to help the needy in Jerusalem in the following scriptures: Romans 15:22-31; 1 Corinthians 16:1-4; 2 Corinthians 8:1-9:15 and in Acts 11:27-30. The funds raised by Paul were to be used to help the Christians and the Jewish Nation! There is no doubt that the early Christians were a benevolent people.

SECOND JEWEL: Saying the right words is no substitute for action, *"Go in peace, be warmed and filled, without giving them the things needed for the body, what good is that?"* James 2:16. How crazy is it to tell a cold and hungry person to *"be warmed and filled"* and then to turn them out with nothing but our good wishes? At times, we humans are so thoughtless! The tendency to be thoughtless manifests itself in many ways. For example, we often tell a person we will pray for them and then we don't. Or, we offer to come by for a visit, and then we don't. Or, we say to the Lord that we will read and study our Bible more often but we don't.

Surely our faces should burn red with embarrassment as we reflect upon our many failures. Let's face it; we sometimes talk much better than we perform. James instructs us to do more than say the right words. He urges us to do the right deeds! By all means, we are to help the needy among us with the things that they need.

THIRD JEWEL: Faith by itself is dead, *"So also faith by itself, if it does not have works, is dead,"* James 2:17. When we say, *"I believe"* and our actions prove otherwise, our faith is dead. This idea will be addressed again in

James 2:26. If you were to find a body lying in the road and stopped to investigate, it would not take you long to determine if the person was dead or alive. So, too, we can look at a person's active obedience and determine if they have faith that is coupled with works. If such is not the case, they are dead. Yes, it is true, faith by itself, is dead.

FOURTH JEWEL: Faith and works cannot stand alone, *"But someone will say, 'You have faith and I have works.' Show me your faith apart from your works, and I will show you my faith by my works,"* James 2:18. This section contains a false claim in regards to faith and works. The claim is *"You have faith and I have works."* This claim suggests that some people have the gift of works and others have the gift of faith. If this claim is true, then it stands to reason that the opposite is true as well. The opposite claim would be, *"I have works and you have faith".* Both assertions are attempts to separate faith and works by claiming they are stand-alone attributes of a Christian.

At first glance this theory seems to make perfect sense. A person might even point to 1 Corinthians 12:4-11 to support the idea that there are different gifts for the people of God. There is no doubt that God gifts people with special abilities. Hence the claim, *"You have faith and I have works"* has the sound of truth. However, as we will see in the following paragraph, the claim is false.

James 2:18 refutes any effort to separate faith and works. This powerful passage states, *"Show me your faith apart from your works, and I will show you my faith by my works."* Faith and works are coupled together as a unit and cannot be separated from each other. We are commanded to show our faith by our works. To do otherwise is to stand apart from the clear teaching of the book of James.

DEMONS BELIEVE AND SHUDDER
James 2:19-20

"You believe that God is one; you do well. Even the demons believe—and shudder! [20] Do you want to be shown, you foolish person, that faith apart from works is useless?"

James presents two powerful truths in these two verses. First he points out the truth that demons really do exist. These spiritual beings believe to the point of shuddering. Demons are the devil's helpers. The devil is not a fairy tale. He is real and has been a subtle tempter of mankind since the days of Adam and Eve. Satan appeared in the wilderness in person in order to tempt the Lord, Jesus Christ, Matthew 4:1-11. The second lesson we learn is that faith apart from works is useless. This passage implies that a person who has faith apart from works is no different from demons who believe. In a way that tells us that faith apart from works is demonic. That is not a pretty picture!

The devil uses all subtlety as he tempts mankind. According to Jesus the devil was a murderer and a liar from the beginning, John 8:44-45. When the devil lies he is merely demonstrating his very character. The devil does believe in God and in Jesus Christ but he is so evil and in such total opposition to all that is good that his faith is of no value.

The devil has many evil angels who work under his leadership. These beings are called demons, evil spirits, angels, and devils. Luke 8:28 records the words of a demon that said, *"What do have you to do with me, Jesus, Son of Most High God? I beg you, do not torment me"*. Yes, the devil and his demons do believe in God and they know their destiny. Even so, they do not have saving faith.

We learn from our text that the faith of the demons is so strong that they shudder, James 2:19. The Greek lexicons define *"shudder"* as *"To bristle, stand on end; to shudder so that the skin becomes rough and pimpled and the hair stands on end."* I am sure they shudder because of the majesty and power of God. They also shudder because of their knowledge of their final destiny. After all, the Bible clearly states that hell is a place of *"eternal fire prepared for the devil and his angels"*, Matthew 25:41.

THE MAN CALLED LEGION

Jesus once met a man in the area of the Decapolis (ten cities) who was possessed by many demons, Luke 8:26-39. The demon possessed man lived in the cemetery, was naked, and had such great strength that when he was caught and bound, he was able to break his bonds and flee into the wilderness. Later he would come back to his home in the cemetery. In those days, I suspect very few people took a walk through the cemetery at night (or any other time)!

When the man came to Jesus the demons spoke to Him and begged the Lord not to command them to depart into the abyss, Luke 8:31. The abyss could refer to the place where angels who sinned were sent, 2 Peter 2:4. Per their request, the Lord allowed the demons to enter a herd of pigs. From Mark 5:12-13 we learn that 2,000 pigs ran over the cliff and were drowned. Some authorities believe that means there were at least 2,000 demons cast out of the man who lived in the cemetery.

No wonder the demons shudder! Their destiny is both severe and eternal. The demons already know what is in store for them in the future. The reason the faith of the demons is mentioned is to prove to us how important it is for faith to issue in good works. This one example should be sufficient to convince us that faith apart from works cannot save us. Christians must show their faith by their works. However, the Holy Spirit saw fit to give even more evidence to prove that faith must have works in order to be saving faith.

THE EXAMPLE OF ABRAHAM
James 2:21-24

"Was not Abraham our father justified by works when he offered up his son Isaac on the altar? 22 You see that faith was active along with his works, and faith was completed by his works; 23 and the Scripture was fulfilled that says, 'Abraham believed God, and it was counted to him as righteousness'—and he was called a friend of God. 24 You see that a person is justified by works and not by faith alone."

Now we move from believing demons to the marvelous faith of Abraham, a man whom God called *"Abraham, my friend,"* Isaiah 41:8. Wow! How is that for a relationship? I cannot think of a more powerful testimony to the life of Abraham than the simple statement that he was God's friend. Paul points out that Abraham believed God and the Lord counted that faith as righteousness, Romans 4:3. According to James 2:21 Abraham was justified by his works. This great man of God had both faith and works.

Genesis 22:1-14 contains the commandment from God for Abraham to offer his son, Isaac on an altar. This commandment would be exceedingly difficult for any loving father to perform. In Abraham's case it was even more difficult because his son was a child of promise. The Nation of Israel was to come through the lineage of Isaac. Christ would come through Abraham and Isaac.

The fact that Abraham obeyed God demonstrated *"that his faith was active along with his works, and faith was completed by his works,"* James 2:22. Abraham's willingness to offer Isaac as a sacrifice was the result of his deep faith in God. He trusted God to fulfill his promises even if it required bringing his son back from the dead.

FIRST JEWEL: Abraham's faith was active. *"You see that faith was active along with his works, and faith was completed by his works* James 2:22. The word *"active"* means, *"work together, in conjunction with"*. Therefore faith and works, in Abraham's life, were inseparable. Faith worked in conjunction with his works. Simply put, God commanded Abraham to do something (offer his son as a sacrifice) and the patriarch believed God and did what he was commanded to do.

SECOND JEWEL: Abraham's faith fulfilled scripture and was counted as righteousness. *"The Scripture was fulfilled that says, 'Abraham believed God, and it was counted to him as righteousness'—and he was called a friend of God,"* James 2:23. This pronouncement of Abraham's righteousness was first announced in Genesis 15:6, an event that took place many years before Isaac was born. According to James, this promise of Genesis 15:6 was fulfilled when Abraham offered his son on the altar, Genesis 22. His faith completed his works. No wonder God called Abraham His friend. From the example of Abraham we can clearly see that a child of God must believe God and be active with his works. Christians today need to follow in his steps.

THIRD JEWEL: Abraham was justified by works and not by faith alone. *"You see that a person is justified by works and not by faith alone,"* James 2:24. The same is true for us today. James says, *"that a person is justified by works"*. Paul wrote, *"We have been justified by faith,"* Romans 5:1. These two passages do not conflict each other, rather, they explain the relationship that exists between faith and works. Faith and works go together like a hand in a glove. They work together. Faith alone cannot bring forth the fruit the Lord demands of us. We must have a faith that works.

Like it or not, Scripture teaches us we are *"justified by works and not by faith alone,"* James 2:24. To be justified means to receive *"a judicial decision to free a man from his guilt (which stands in the way of his being right) and to represent him as righteous"*. I read somewhere that to be justified is to have a relationship with God that makes us stand before Him just as if we had never sinned.

THE EXAMPLE OF RAHAB, James 2:25-26

"And in the same way was not also Rahab the prostitute justified by works when she received the messengers and sent them out by another way? [26] *For as the body apart from the spirit is dead, so also faith apart from works is dead."*

The story of Rahab gives us our final example of faith that issues in works. Read Joshua 6:1-27 to learn the story of Rahab. When the Israelite spies came to her house, she believed the Israelites were blessed of God and that they would despoil her city and the entire land of Canaan. As a result she hid the spies and sent them out another way. She also pled with them for deliverance for her and her family. God blessed this woman because of her faith and her works.

This believing woman married Salmon, an Israelite from the tribe of Judah, who had a son named Boaz who in married Ruth, the Moabite. Both Rahab and Ruth are women who are listed in the lineage of Jesus, Matthew 1:5. King David was also an offspring from these godly women, Ruth 4:18-21. Who would have thought that Rahab, a woman who is called a prostitute, would be chosen to be one of the people of faith who would be found in the lineage of Jesus, the Christ?

From the example of Rahab we learn that having a faith that works is a matter of life or death. That is a startling truth! This is true concerning the spies whose lives were spared because of the works of Rahab. *"She received the messengers and sent them out by another way,"* James 2:25. It was also true that the good works of Rahab saved the lives of her family members when Jericho fell to the Israelites. The most important thing is that Rahab became a believer in God who demonstrated her faith by her works. The strongest statement in the entire chapter to describe faith and works is used in the story of Rahab.

LIFE REQUIRES BOTH BODY AND SPIRIT

When God created man he formed him *"from the dust of the ground and breathed into his nostrils the breath (spirit) of life and man became a living creature"*, Genesis 2:7. Some translations of the Bible say, *"man became a living soul"*. We all understand when a man dies, his soul departs from his body and he dies. Speaking of death, Solomon wrote, *"The dust* (body of man) *returns to the earth as it was, and the spirit returns to God who gave it,"* Ecclesiastes 12:7.

Rachel died giving birth to Benjamin. The Bible record states, *"Her soul was departing (for she was dying), she called his name Ben-oni but his father called him Benjamin. So Rachael died and she was buried, "* Genesis 35:18-19. Amazingly, James compares physical life to spiritual life. *"For as the body apart from the spirit is dead, so also faith apart from works is dead."* Just as a person dies physically when the spirit leaves his body, so a person of faith dies if his life does not issue in works.

Once we are dead physically we can no longer do anything in this world. We are eternally separated from other mortal beings. Since faith apart from works is also dead, it only stands to reason that such a person no longer has a functioning Christian life. He is dead.

We all need to find a place in the kingdom where we can exercise an active faith that demonstrates it's life by working for the cause of Christ. When our work on earth is accomplished, God will call us to our heavenly home where we will spend eternity with Him. What a glorious day that will be!

DISCUSSION QUESTIONS:

1. Discuss how we could do a better job of helping the needy. Include ideas on helping needy Christians among us and on helping needy people in the world. Consider the teaching found in Galatians 6:10.

2. Discuss the passages given in this chapter that show the First Century Christians were a benevolent people.

3. Discuss the four *"jewels"* listed under the topic **Helping The Needy**.

4. Discuss the section on demons. Do you think demons are active today? Discuss Ephesians 6:12 in your answer.

5. Discuss the three *"jewels"* under **The Example of Abraham**.

6. What event fulfilled the promise of God to Abraham that is found in Genesis 15:6?

7. Discuss the meaning of James 2:26.

Chapter 8

DANGERS OF THE TONGUE
James 3:1-11

James 3:1
"Not many of you should become teachers, my brothers, for you know that we who teach will be judged with greater strictness."

TEACHERS AND THEIR WORDS

We are now introduced to James' discussion on the tongue with a scathing denunciation against teachers who do not control their tongues. His stern warning could very well discourage many from wanting to teach the word of God. Many people have questioned me over the years asking me why James began his discussion on tongues in such a negative way. After all, most congregations are on the constant lookout for more teachers. Why discourage people from the task of teaching the word of God?

Here we are warned that not many should become teachers. He adds that those who teach will *"be judged with greater strictness"*. The reason for this stern warning could be because teachers use their *"tongues"* to instruct others. To give a stern warning is justified because the destiny of men's souls is at stake. Standing before others to declare, *"thus says the Lord"* is an awesome and serious responsibility.

FIRST JEWEL: Teachers need proper knowledge. Paul warned Timothy about people who wanted to teach but were ignorant of their subject matter. *"The aim of our charge is love that issues from a pure heart and a good conscience and a sincere faith. Certain persons, by swerving from these, have wandered away into vain discussion, desiring to be teachers of the law, without understanding either what they are saying or the things about which they make confident assertions,"* 1

Timothy 1:5-7. It is imperative for us to be able to teach the inspired Word of God accurately. This is only possible when one is a diligent student of the word. Teachers must develop their teaching skills so they can lead their students towards learning the meaning of scripture and in order to lead them in the direction God would have them to go. Therefore a warning to teachers is justified.

SECOND JEWEL: Teachers' words will judge them. Jesus clearly taught the need to choose our words carefully. *"Either make the tree good and its fruit good, or make the tree bad and its fruit bad, for the tree is known by its fruit. You brood of vipers! How can you speak good, when you are evil? For out of the abundance of the heart the mouth speaks. The good person out of his good treasure brings forth good, and the evil person out of his evil treasure brings forth evil. I tell you, on the day of judgment people will give account for every careless word they speak, for by your words you will be justified, and by your words you will be condemned,"* Matthew 12:33–37. Careless words from the mouths of teachers can impact the lives of their students in a negative way. Teachers and students alike will be judged by the words that come out of their mouths. What we say will either justify us or condemn us.

It is difficult to speak right words effectively if we are not *"practicing what we preach"*. A teacher who does not live the message he proclaims will have to answer to God for that failure. In addition, those who really know the teacher won't put much stock in what is said if the speaker is living differently than the message he teaches. Teachers must understand that they will be judged with "greater *strictness*" in regard to their lifestyle as well as their words.

THIRD JEWEL: Teacher's must use gracious words. I wonder how many people are turned away from obeying the Gospel because of the attitude displayed by the person presenting the truth? Can you see how important it is to be gracious with your words when you teach others? *"Let your speech always be gracious, seasoned with salt, so that you may know how you ought to answer each person,"* Colossians 4:6. It would be a terrible tragedy to teach the truth in such a manner that the listener is turned away from obedience instead of being brought closer to the Lord.

The word gracious comes from a Greek word meaning *"a kind, affectionate, pleasing nature and inclining disposition . . . beauty of speech"*. It is not sufficient just to be right – you must also be gracious. The teacher's ability to speak gracious words helps us to understand what was meant in James 1:26 where we learned that a religious man who does not bridle his tongue has *"deceived his heart, this person's religion is worthless"*. The need to use gracious words applies to everyone but it has a special meaning to those of us who stand before others teaching the word of the Lord. Is it any wonder that those who teach will be judged with greater strictness? After all, the words we speak not only affect our own destiny but they also affect the destiny of those who hear us. Yes, it is true, teaching good and true words can save both the teachers and their students alike, 1 Timothy 4:17.

THE TONGUE CAN BE A DEADLY EVIL!
James 3:2-6

"For we all stumble in many ways, and if anyone does not stumble in what he says, he is a perfect man, able also to bridle his whole body. ³ If we put bits into the mouths of horses so that they obey us, we guide their whole bodies as well. ⁴ Look at the ships also: though they are so large and are driven by strong winds, they are guided by a very small rudder wherever the will of the pilot directs. ⁵ So also the tongue is a small member, yet it boasts of great things. How great a forest is set ablaze by such a small fire! ⁶ And the tongue is a fire, a world of unrighteousness. The tongue is set among our members, staining the whole body, setting on fire the entire course of life, and set on fire by hell."

These verses clearly show the propensity of mankind to stumble and fall because of the words that come out of their mouths. When a child of God has a sinful tongue he reveals an inconsistency in his life that could lead him to destruction. *"For we all stumble in many ways, and if anyone does not stumble in what he says, he is a perfect man, able also to bridle his whole body."* Of course, the tongue is not the only lifestyle inconsistency that leads us to spiritual trouble but it is a leading source of difficulty for us all.

INCONSISTENCIES LEAD TO TROUBLES

As an example of inconsistency in the life of God's people let's look at the Nation of Israel from the book of Judges. This illustration is appropriate in the context of studying problems of the tongue. *"For we all stumble in many ways, and if anyone does not stumble in what he says, he is a perfect man, able also to bridle his whole body,"* James 3:2. During this period of history when Israel was faithful God blessed them just like He promised He would. After a period of time the people slowly fell away from faithful service to the Lord. Because of their inconsistencies and sinful practices God would raise up a nearby Nation to conquer Israel and subject them to difficult servitude. The purpose of their difficult times was to bring Israel back to faithful service to God. As time passed, Israel would fall on their knees in repentance and offer prayers to the Lord for their deliverance. As a result of their repentance, Jehovah God would raise up a judge to deliver them from their oppressors. Once again the Israelites would worship God and enjoy prosperity in the land of Canaan.

There were fifteen judges all together. The first judge was Othniel and the last was Samuel. After turning from their sins and being restored to freedom and prosperity the children of Israel tragically repeated their inconsistent lifestyle and sinned against God. A heathen Nation once again rose up and oppressed Israel. This pattern became a cycle that repeated itself over and over again in the book of Judges. People today are much like the ancient Israelites. It is so easy to rejoice in blessings God has given us only to carelessly stumble and fall away from our faithfulness to the Lord. The story of Israel and the judges deals with sinful lifestyles and the sad state of God's people when they turn away from serving the Lord.

We are studying inconsistencies of the tongue. All too often our problems begin with our tongues and are followed up by our sinful actions. With our tongues we promise much but by our actions we often deliver much less. Don't be deceived. God will not bless us if we don't control our tongues. He will allow us to become slaves of sin and serve under the oppression of the devil.

THE POWER OF THE TONGUE

FIRST JEWEL: Tongue control equals perfection. *"For we all stumble in many ways, and if anyone does not stumble in what he says, he is a perfect man, able also to bridle his whole body,"* James 3:2. The Greek word, *"perfect"* in James 3:2 means to be mature. We studied the word perfect in an earlier chapter and learned it never means sinless perfection. If it did we all would be lost. James describes the man who controls his tongue as a perfect (mature) man, one who will not stumble in what he says. This person has bridled his whole body and is ready for fruitful service in God's kingdom.

How many times has your tongue gotten you into trouble? If you are like me you probably don't want to answer that question. No one controls his tongue all of the time. However, far too many of us excuse our lack of tongue control by quoting James who said, *"No human being can tame the tongue,"* James 3:8. When we study that verse we will learn what it really means.

Do not be deceived. God will not overlook the words we speak. Don't forget, some words are spoken only in our minds yet they are still our words. Do you think those words spoken only in our minds will count? Yes, they will. We will be held accountable for what we say out loud and what we say silently in our minds.

SECOND JEWEL: A bit in a horse's mouth. *"If we put bits into the mouths of horses so that they obey us, we guide their whole bodies as well,"* James 3:3. I was raised in the city. As I grew up I seldom visited people living in the countryside. Consequently, I had a lack of knowledge on how it was to live on a ranch. I seldom rode a horse but I did see lots of Western movies.

Back in the 50's, I learned about the importance of a bit and bridle on a horse. While on a visit to my cousin's ranch in Uvalde, Texas I wanted to ride a horse and I was very impatient about it. I wanted to ride that horse *"right now!"* The horse I wanted to ride was slowly eating its oats. Impatiently, I pulled him away from his dinner, saddled him up and rode off into the sunset. Or, so I thought!

Once on the horse's back I kicked him in the side. This rather small animal launched into a full gallop with me barely hanging on. He bowed his neck and the reigns were jerked right out of my hands. At that moment I lost what little control I had over this animal! I was hanging onto the saddle horn praying that I could stay onboard. My steed evidently saw some beans growing on a mesquite tree just ahead and he stopped very suddenly so that he could eat them. Well, I didn't stop at all! I flew through the air until I fell to the ground with a thud and slid to a painful halt.

Every time I look at James chapter three I remember what happened to me on my uncle's ranch in Uvalde. The tongue is likened unto a horse that needs a bit inserted into his mouth so that his rider can guide his whole body. Though the horse is larger and more powerful than we are, with a bit and a bridle, we can control his entire body. He will go exactly where we want him to go.

The tongue is just like that. If we lose control of our tongues our lives will soon get out of control. We are headed towards spiritual disaster. Without a bit we will lose control very quickly. As a result we will come down to earth with a thud and slide to a painful halt!

THIRD JEWEL: The tongue as a ship's rudder. *"Look at the ships also: though they are so large and are driven by strong winds, they are guided by a very small rudder wherever the will of the pilot directs* [5] *So also the tongue is a small member, yet it boasts of great things,"* James 3:4-5a. Having been in the United States Navy, I fully understand how a rudder can control a huge Navy vessel. I once served on the crew of the USS Columbus, CG5. This huge cruiser had many levels. The conning tower was perched high above the main deck. There were multiple levels under the water line. With a full complement of sailors we could have 800± crewmembers stationed onboard. In proportion to the size of our Naval vessel the rudder was very small. Yet it guided the ship unswervingly in the direction it needed to go. When we follow our Lord's instructions our rudder will guide us correctly and we will arrive at our proper destination. Otherwise we are certain to get off course.

Don't you marvel at how small the tongue is? Yet it boasts of great things! Far too often we use our tongue to glorify ourselves and to boast about our own abilities rather than to glorify God. Too often we boast of our *"great"* achievements instead of giving God the glory. Great servants of the Lord seek God's approval not man's. *"For am I now seeking the approval of man, or of God? Or am I trying to please man? If I were still trying to please man, I would not be a servant of Christ,"* Galatians 1:10. The Bible presents a better way of living by saying, *"Let the one who boasts, boast in the Lord,"* 1 Corinthians 1:31.

FOURTH JEWEL: The tongue as a destructive fire. *"How great a forest is set ablaze by such a small fire! And the tongue is a fire, a world of unrighteousness. The tongue is set among our members, staining the whole body, setting on fire the entire course of life, and set on fire by hell,"* James 3:5b-6. Every year America burns! The number of acres burned during the year 2012, as of November 22, was 9.87 million acres or over 15,000 square miles. This was the third highest number of acres burned since National wildfire statistics have been kept (beginning in 1960). To put that into perspective, that is the same as burning the entire landmass of New Hampshire and Hawaii combined!

Misuse of the tongue starts out small but before long it gets completely out of control. Such a tongue is likened unto a great forest fire blazing out of control. Just as a small insignificant cigarette butt thrown out of the window of a car can spread into a raging fire that damages property and costs the lives of many people, so the tongue can bring about great devastation, not only to self but also to others.

Such a tongue stains the whole body and it affects the course of one's life. An uncontrolled tongue is set on fire by hell (gehenna in the Greek). As we learned earlier, hell is a place intended for the devil and his angels. It is a shame so many people will join the devil in the lake of fire. Sadly, the tongue will lead many to the devil's final dwelling place. An uncontrolled tongue is not heavenly; it is devilish. It is inconsistent with the lifestyle God would have us to live.

TAMING THE TONGUE
James 3:7-12

"For every kind of beast and bird, of reptile and sea creature, can be tamed and has been tamed by mankind, ⁸ but no human being can tame the tongue. It is a restless evil, full of deadly poison. ⁹ With it we bless our Lord and Father, and with it we curse people who are made in the likeness of God. ¹⁰ From the same mouth come blessing and cursing. My brothers, these things ought not to be so. ¹¹ Does a spring pour forth from the same opening both fresh and salt water? ¹² Can a fig tree, my brothers, bear olives, or a grapevine produce figs? Neither can a salt pond yield fresh water."

Can a man *"tame"* his tongue? The word *"tame"* in the Greek means *"to overpower, to subdue"*. The word is used in Mark 5:4 in reference to the man possessed with a legion of demons. He was wild, he was naked, and he could not be tamed. In the book of Mark the ESV uses the English word *"subdued"* but it is the exact same Greek word translated *"tamed"* in James 3:7.

What does scripture mean when it says, *"But no human being can tame the tongue. It is a restless evil, full of deadly poison,"* James 3:8? There are two possibilities. Some say this verse means that you cannot tame your own tongue. The tongue is called a *"restless evil, full of deadly poison"*. It is thought that man's tongue is such that only God can tame it. Man cannot do it himself. Therefore, it is through prayer and the help of God that an uncontrolled tongue must be tamed. This interpretation sounds good but is in conflict with James 1:26, *"If anyone thinks he is religious and does not bridle his tongue but deceives his heart, this person's religion is worthless"*. This verse teaches us that each individual has a personal responsibility to bridle his own tongue.

Others believe this verse teaches that we cannot tame another man's tongue in the same way we might tame an animal to do our bidding. This interpretation emphasizes tongue control as a job for each individual to accomplish for himself. I cannot control your tongue and you cannot control mine. However, each person is responsible for controlling the words that come out of his own mouth. This author believes this interpretation of James 3:8 is more plausible. Of course, we still need help from God above in order to become successful.

Here is the context. *"For every kind of beast and bird, of reptile and sea creature, can be tamed and has been tamed by mankind, but no human being can tame the tongue. It is a restless evil, full of deadly poison,"* James 3:7-8. We were given dominion over the animals, Genesis 1:26, so we can control them and train them to do many things. It is amazing that some birds can be taught to imitate human speech. I recently saw a dog on television imitating human speech imitating the words *"I love you"*. He was barking softly but it definitely sounded like human speech! We have dominion over the animals and have trained them to do many amazing things.

We do not have the same power over our fellow man. What is being said in this context is that while I can control animals I cannot tame your tongue. That is your own personal responsibility. However, I can (and must) learn to tame my own speech. If I don't learn how to do this my religion is worthless, James 1:26.

INCONSISTENCIES OF THE TONGUE

FIRST JEWEL: Blessing and cursing. *"With it* (our tongue) *we bless our Lord and Father, and with it we curse people who are made in the likeness of God. From the same mouth come blessing and cursing. My brothers, these things ought not to be so"*, James 3:9-10. Some would call this type of speech *"talking out of* *both sides of your mouth".* In 1 John 4:20-21 we learn that it is not proper to claim to love God while hating our brother. A man who says those words is a liar. John concluded with the words, *"This commandment we have from him: whoever loves God must also love his brother."* It is important to be consistent in our words and not to bless God and curse man from the same mouth.

SECOND JEWEL: A fresh water spring. *"Does a spring pour forth from the same opening both fresh and salt water?"* James 3:11. The laws of nature put in force by the living God make it impossible for a spring to bring forth fresh and salt water at the same time. But we human beings, who were created in the image of God, often bless God and curse each other in the same sentence! *"From the same mouth come blessing and cursing. My brothers, these things ought not to be so,"* James 3:10. God made man with the power of choice. For this reason we can easily become double minded and speak unadvisedly with our lips.

THIRD JEWEL: The reliability of seed. *"Can a fig tree, my brothers, bear olives, or a grapevine produce figs?"* James 3:12a. Seed produces after its own kind, Genesis 1:12. Fig trees bear figs – not olives. Grapevines produce grapes – not figs. When you plant seed it always brings forth the right kind of plant. I once saw a movie where two men bought seed for their garden out of the back of a salesman's truck. They thought they had many different kinds of seed but they didn't. They were inexperienced farmers and trusted the salesman to give them what they asked for. When the seeds came forth all they had was corn. Each package contained the picture of different vegetables but the seed was not as advertised. We know that seed is consistent. It always brings forth after its own kind. The human tongue is far less reliable. We can bless God and curse man at the same time.

FOURTH JEWEL: The reliability of a salt pond. *"Neither can a salt pond yield fresh water,"* James 3:12. A salt pond cannot produce fresh water. One taste and you will know what kind of water you are drinking. If it is a salt pond you will not want to drink any more water from that pond because you know it will never produce fresh water. But, if it is a fresh water pond, you will gladly refresh yourself with a cool drink of water anytime that you can.

Man, needs to learn to control his tongue. As children of God we should, follow the advice of the Psalmist. *"I said, I will guard my ways, that I may not sin with my tongue,"* Psalm 39:1. You can learn more on the damage an uncontrolled tongue can do by using your Bible concordance to do a word study on words related to man's speech. Look up the following words: tongue, pride, lying, lips, mouth, and speech. If you want, you can make your own list. You will find it to be an enlightening study.

It seems only natural that a discussion on the tongue would be followed by a comparison of true and false wisdom. That will be our discussion in our next chapter.

DISCUSSION QUESTIONS:

1. Discuss the section in this chapter dealing with teachers. What can we do to help people to become teachers of the word of God?

2. Discuss the idea that inconsistencies in the words we say can lead to troubles in our lives.

3. The section on the **POWER OF THE TONGUE** contained four *"jewels"*. Discuss each of them and discover ideas from them that will help us have control over our tongue.

4. Discuss James 3:8, *"No human being can tame the tongue"*. What does it mean?

5. Discuss the four "jewels" listed under the heading **INCONSISTENCIES OF THE TONGUE.**

> # Chapter 9

TRUE AND FALSE WISDOM
LEARNING THE DIFFERENCE
James 3:13-18

James 3:13
"Who is wise and understanding among you? By his good conduct let him show his works in the meekness of wisdom."

GOD'S WISE MEN

Before looking at the text of James 3:13-18 it would be good to discuss the different kinds of wise men found in the Bible. They are an important group of godly servants who appeared throughout the history of mankind. There were different kinds of wise men with each group having different levels of service. Each group served a vital role in helping the community to live a godly life that was acceptable to Jehovah God. It was important for these men to be available to the people so they could offer good advice and counsel to those who were facing difficult situations in their lives.

LAWGIVER: Moses stands in a unique class by himself, Deuteronomy 34:9-12. In this passage Moses is presented as a one-of-a-kind servant of the Most High. There was no other man like Moses whom God knew and to whom He spoke face-to-face. God showed great miraculous signs through Moses to both the children of Israel and to their task masters, the Egyptians. Deuteronomy 18:15-18 informs us that he was also a uniquely gifted prophet. This passage contains the promise that another prophet like Moses would appear in the future. Jesus Christ is the fulfillment of that promise, Acts 3:22-23.

As the leader of God's people and as a wise man, Moses settled disputes among the Israelites. They all knew he was filled with wisdom that came from God. Of course, he also received and wrote down the laws and ordinances God designed for the Nation of Israel. In addition, Moses wrote the first five books of the Old Testament.

PROPHETS/SEERS: The prophets had the important responsibility to communicate to Israel the divine word of God. Micah said his work was *"to declare to Jacob his transgression and to Israel his sin,"* Micah 3:8. In 1 Samuel 9:9 we learn the office of seer and prophet are exactly the same office. God chose and inspired his prophets through the Holy Spirit. They were charged to deliver God's message to the people.

Because their task was to rebuke the Nation for their sins and to warn them of coming disasters, they were often despised and mistreated by the people they served. The world was not worthy of these great men of God, Hebrews 11:38. Not all of the prophets were writing prophets. The books produced by the writing prophets, at least the books God intended for us to have, are included in the canon of scripture. The Holy Spirit inspired every prophet of God whether he wrote a book or not. It is this author's conviction that every author of every single book in the Bible was a prophet of God even though he might serve in other areas of leadership as well. For example, David was a king and a prophet, Acts 2:30.

PRIESTS: The priests of the Old Testament, sons of Aaron, were charged with a two-fold responsibility. Their first function was to teach and interpret the Law. In Israel there was both civil and ecclesiastical law. Their second function was to offer the different kinds of sacrifices God required of the Israelites.

When the priests failed to teach the Law, Israel became ignorant of God's righteous requirements. The children of Israel often suffered at the hands of their enemies as punishment for departing from the commandments of Jehovah God. You can read about the failure of the priests to teach the word of God in Hosea 4:6-9. Here is a portion of that passage. *"My people are destroyed for lack of knowledge; because you have rejected knowledge, I reject you from being a priest to me . . . . and it shall be like people, like priest; I will punish them for their ways and repay them for their deeds."*

Anytime religious teachers fail to teach the word of the Lord the people will became ignorant and sinful. One consequence of sin is the loss of

God's blessings. Even though we live under the Christian age God has not changed. He will still punish those who claim to be His people when they turn away from His commandments. *"Note then the kindness and the severity of God: severity towards those who have fallen, but God's kindness to you, provided you continue in his kindness. Otherwise you too will be cut off,"* Romans 11:22.

POETS/PSALMISTS: These men wrote the Wisdom Literature of the Bible (Job, Psalms, Proverbs, Ecclesiastes, and Song of Solomon). All of these books were written in the style of Hebrew poetry. David wrote many of the Psalms but there were at least eight other authors as well. We do not know who authored many of the Psalms.

In the Psalms (150 separate books altogether) we can read expressions of the deepest emotions of mankind. The Psalms seek to glorify God and express a deep faith that the Lord will carry them through the trials and tribulations of life. Others give praise to God as creator and sustainer of all things. Some of the Psalmists foretold future events including prophecies of the coming Messiah. All of the Wisdom Literature is valuable for personal study and reflection.

The wise men that wrote the Wisdom Literature truly gave the world many marvelous teachings. The Psalms can calm the trouble soul as well as help express a deep and abiding faith in God and His word. The book of Proverbs provides us with many wise sayings from Godly men of the era. Even though Solomon wrote the majority of the book, he was not the only author of Proverbs. Some parts of the book contains the sayings of the other wise men including Agur, son of Jakeh, Proverbs 30:1 and King Lemuel, Proverbs 31:1. It is possible that Solomon collected these men's sayings and included them along with his own writings.

JUDGES: After Israel conquered the Promised Land they were served by fifteen men who served as judges. Read about them in the book of Judges and 1 Samuel. We discussed this class of leader in the previous chapter of this book. To refresh your memory you might want to turn back and read that section again.

The judge served as leader and wise counselor for the people. He served in this capacity for his entire lifetime. Usually, sometime after his death, the people would again depart from the commandments of the Lord and the cycle would repeat itself. When Saul was anointed as the first King of Israel the period of the judges began to come to an end.

WISE MEN AND WOMEN: Two of the wise men that served King David during his reign were Ahithophel and Hushai. The former is mentioned several times in 2 Samuel chapters 15 through 17. When this wise man spoke it seemed to the people, *"as if one consulted the word of God; so was all the counsel of Ahithophel esteemed,"* 2 Samuel 16:23. When David's son, Absalom, attempted to ascend to the throne of Israel, this wise man became his advisor and betrayed King David. Because his counsel to attack King David and his men was rejected in favor of the advice given by Hushai, another wise man, Ahithophel took his own life. Many other wise men appear in the pages of both the Old and New Testaments.

Deborah was a woman of wisdom who judged the people during the oppression of the Canaanites. *"She used to sit under the palm of Deborah between Ramah and Bethel in the hill country of Ephraim, and the people of Israel came up to her for judgment,"* Judges 4:5. She and Barak delivered the people from their enemies and the land had rest for forty years.

Another woman of wisdom was an unnamed woman mentioned in 2 Samuel 20:16-22. She counseled Joab not to destroy the city of Abel of Beth-maacah as he sought to kill a rebel named Sheba. Her counsel was not to destroy a city when the head of one man would serve the same purpose. With the approval of Joab, she went to all the people in her wisdom to persuade them to kill Sheba, the son of Bichri in order to save the city. Her wise words saved the lives of many people.

APOSTLES: In the New Testament we have the wisdom of Jesus' Apostles. They were men who followed Jesus throughout His personal ministry. Jesus appointed them to be Apostles in Matthew 10:2-4. The word *"Apostle"* means *one sent, messenger, ambassador, envoy"*. Some describe an Apostle as *"one sent with orders"*. Paul was also appointed to be an Apostle even though he was not a disciple of Jesus during His lifetime. Paul received his training from Jesus while in Arabia, Galatians 1:11-17.

After His death every one of Jesus' Apostles were inspired by the Holy Spirit so they could preach the whole counsel of God. With the Spirit's help they were able to remember everything Jesus taught them. The Spirit continued to teach them all the things they needed to know in order to accomplish their ministry. The Spirit guided the Apostles to all truth and showed them future events that were yet to come. Read John 14:25-26 and 16:12-13 for details on the Divine help given to these wise men of God. Some of the Apostles continue to bless us today through the New Testament books they wrote. Matthew, John, Peter, and Paul wrote books of the New Testament. As with all of the books of the Bible, the Apostles wrote by the inspiration of the Holy Spirit.

CHURCH LEADERS: The Bible tells us that God gave the church different kinds of church leaders to help us grow in faith. The book of Philippians provides us a list of some of those leadership positions. *"Paul and Timothy, servants of Christ Jesus to all the saints in Christ Jesus who are at Philippi, with the overseers and deacons,"* Philippians 1:1. Look over this verse to discover the office of an apostle (Paul), an evangelist (Timothy), overseers (Elders), and deacons (servants of the church). The verse also mentions saints, a word that describes members of the body of Christ in the city of Philippi.

Many of these types of church leaders continue to serve the church as today's wise men. They are able to give us good counsel from the word of God. They do so by sharing their knowledge of the Bible and by using the wisdom given to them by God. Churches that are organized in accordance to the pattern found in the New Testament are able to tap the wisdom of modern day wise men of God.

GODLY AND EARTHLY WISDOM
James 3:13
"Who is wise and understanding among you? By his good conduct let him show his works in the meekness of wisdom."

Many people seek to find true wisdom to live by. Yet, not all wisdom is the same. Is that confusing? Not if you understand there are two kinds of wisdom. (See our discussion in **Chapter Two** under James 1:5-8 under the heading **"Acquiring Wisdom"** for a review of the meaning of wisdom.) From that chapter we learned, among other things, that wisdom is the ability to use knowledge. Our responsibility is to gain knowledge. Then, when we ask, in faith, God will grant us godly wisdom, which is the better of the two kinds of wisdom. The second kind of wisdom is called *"earthly* *wisdom"*. It looks good on the outside but it is unable to discern the spiritual truths that are revealed in the Bible.

James asked the question, *"Who is wise among you?"* He is speaking of wise people among the believers. Truly the church needs people who have wisdom and understanding to lead us in the ways of the Lord. After studying James 3:13-18 we should be able to see the difference between the wisdom from above and earthly wisdom.

FIRST JEWEL: Godly wisdom produces good conduct, *"Who is wise and understanding among you? By his good conduct let him show his works in the meekness of wisdom,"* James 3:13. The true measure of godly wisdom is not what we say but what we do. We show others our wisdom by our good conduct and by the works we do in meekness of wisdom. By demonstrating these characteristics others can see our wisdom.

Solomon was the wisest man of his age. Many believe that, in the history of mankind, only Jesus had more wisdom than Solomon. Early in his reign, King Solomon made a judgment between two mothers who had given birth to a child. One infant died and both mothers claimed the living child as their own, 1 Kings 3:16-28. After rendering a wise judgment that returned the living child to his real mother the people *"stood in awe of the king, because they perceived that the wisdom of God was in him to do justice,"* 1 Kings 3:28. Can you see how his wisdom was shown by his good conduct and by his wise decision (works done in meekness of wisdom)?

Solomon's wisdom was far beyond that of other wise men of his era. The queen of Sheba heard of the King's wisdom and made a long journey to Israel in order to determine for herself if Solomon was as wise as she had heard. She left Jerusalem saying, *"The report was true that I heard in my own country of your words and of your wisdom, but I did not believe the reports until I came and my own eyes had seen it. And behold, the half was not told me. Your wisdom and prosperity surpass the report that I heard"* 1 Kings 10:6-7. Godly wisdom makes itself apparent by the good manner of life (good conduct) and by the caliber of the works done.

SECOND JEWEL: Meekness of wisdom. Meekness is a very important character trait for the wise man of God. The Greek word for meekness means: *"gentle, enduring all things with an even temper, tender, free from* *haughty self-sufficiency. . . tenderness in bearing with others"*. Possessing meekness of wisdom will eliminate boasting or arrogance entirely. Wise men show their prowess in a way that honors God and downplays their abilities.

One that is truly wise does not feel the need to tell others about his abilities. Over the years I have observed that before long people just know whom they need to go to when they have a problem or when they need advice. A person filled with God's wisdom doesn't have to hang out a shingle advertising his wisdom. His good conduct, his works, and his meekness of wisdom declare to others, *"Here is a wise man of God"*. His godly lifestyle calls people to him for advice.

ATTRIBUTES OF EARTHLY WISDOM
James 3:14-16
"But if you have bitter jealousy and selfish ambition in your hearts, do not boast and be false to the truth. ¹⁵ This is not the wisdom that comes down from above, but is earthly, unspiritual, demonic. ¹⁶ For where jealousy and selfish ambition exist, there will be disorder and every vile practice."

Some might argue that earthly wisdom comes from God too. To some degree a case could be made for this because the bible does teach that God is the giver of all good gifts, James 1:17. However, the earthly wisdom found in James 3:14-16 is not a good gift. This kind of wisdom leaves God out of the picture altogether. Therefore it is not good and did not come from the Lord.

Many philosophers and educators of higher learning deny the existence of God and the Divinity of Jesus Christ. In their wisdom, there is no need for God nor is there any value to be found in the Holy Bible. A considerable number of the worldly wise men of today consider religion to be a relic from the past that has no measureable benefit for modern man. They certainly do not consider the commandments found in Scripture to be binding upon people in today's world.

There are also religious leaders that have the wrong kind of wisdom. Most of the religious leaders of Jesus' day were considered to be wise but they rejected the only begotten Son of God. They, in spite of their vestments, their position, and their knowledge of the Old Testament, were lacking in godly wisdom. Earthly wisdom is based upon human intelligence and reasoning. It has characteristics that did not come from God but from the evil one.

GODLY AND WORLDLY WISDOM

To enhance our study of James 3:13-17 we will take a brief look at the teaching found in 1 Corinthians 1:18-31. In this passage the Apostle Paul discusses the fallacy of worldly wisdom, a term that describes the same type of wisdom James calls earthly wisdom.

Worldly wisdom does not know God. Paul informs us that the world in its wisdom does not know God, 1 Corinthians 1:21. They should know Him because there is evidence of His existence everywhere. There is evidence from nature, *"The heavens declare the glory of God and the sky above proclaims his handiwork"*, Psalm 19:1. There is evidence from Jesus and His miracles. *"Do you not believe that I am in the Father and the Father is in me? Believe me that I am in the Father and the Father is in me, or else believe on account of the works themselves"* John 14:10-11. The evidence for believing in God is overwhelming yet the one who depends upon worldly wisdom does not, and often cannot, know God.

Worldly wisdom counts God's wisdom to be foolishness, According to 1 Corinthians 1:22-25, the Jews of Paul's day sought signs and the Gentiles sought wisdom. The preaching of Christ and Him crucified became a stumbling block to the people of that era. They should have sought, *"Christ the power of God and the wisdom of God. For the foolishness of God is wiser than men, and the weakness of God is stronger than men,"* 1 Corinthians 1:24-25. To them, the gospel message showed weakness. The difference between worldly and godly wisdom is so vast that it can only be bridged by faith in God and His word.

Worldly wisdom usually rejects God's message, 1 Corinthians 1:26-29. The worldly wise see God's message of salvation as foolishness and weakness. For that reason, not many *"powerful, not many were of noble birth"* fall on their knees before the God of heaven asking, *"What shall we do* (to be saved)? Acts 16:30. God, in His wisdom chose what is low and despised in the world so men could not boast in His presence. A believer must be humbled in order to become a child of God. It is difficult for the worldly wise to admit there is a Supreme Being who has wisdom that is far above what is available to man.

Worldly wisdom rejects the source of life, 1 Corinthians 1:30-31. God is the source of our life in Christ Jesus. For the Christian, Jesus Christ becomes our wisdom, our righteousness, our sanctification and our redemption. Paul's conclusion is *"Let the one who boasts, boast in the Lord,"* 1 Corinthians 1:31. Now we are ready to look at the attributes of the earthly wisdom found in the book of James.

EARTHLY WISDOM DEFINED
James 3:14-16

"But if you have bitter jealousy and selfish ambition in your hearts, do not boast and be false to the truth. 15 This is not the wisdom that comes down from above, but is earthly, unspiritual, demonic. 16 For where jealousy and selfish ambition exist, there will be disorder and every vile practice."

Earthly wisdom is made known by its characteristics. This is the wisdom that comes from the men who do not know God and who reject His holy word. This type of wisdom is described to us as being *"earthly"*. The characteristics of earthly wisdom stand in stark contrast to the godly wisdom that comes from above.

Earthly wisdom is described by the following words:
1. Bitter jealousy
2. Selfish ambition
3. Boastfulness
4. False to truth
5. Earthly
6. Unspiritual
7. Demonic
8. Jealous
9. Selfish ambition

The result of worldly wisdom is disorder and every vile practice. The term *"earthly wisdom"* is used in order to let us know that it comes from man and not from God. The term *"world"* is used in 1 John 2:15 to portray the same meaning. *"Love not the world or the things in the world."* Obviously we can love the physical universe that God created. We cannot love the ungodly sinful practices of the world. Such things are earthly or worldly and they stand in opposition to the wisdom that comes from above. The child of God must reject worldly wisdom in favor of heavenly wisdom; the kind that comes Jehovah God.

THE WISDOM FROM ABOVE
James 3:17-18

"But the wisdom from above is first pure, then peaceable, gentle, open to reason, full of mercy and good fruits, impartial and sincere. [18] And a harvest of righteousness is sown in peace by those who make peace."

God is the source of godly wisdom. He gives that wisdom to faithful people when they ask for it in faith nothing doubting. Prayer is the avenue for receiving it. It is the only wisdom that is able to lead us to eternal life. In contrast to earthly wisdom, the wisdom from above brings forth a harvest of righteousness in those who have received it. This wisdom contains many positive and helpful attributes.

The wisdom from above is described by the following words:

1. Pure
2. Peaceable
3. Gentle
4. Open to reason
5. Full of mercy
6. Good Fruits
7. Impartial
8. Sincere

It is obvious that the two types of wisdom being discussed in this chapter are totally incompatible with each other. When one has the wisdom that comes from God, his life will exhibit the eight characteristics listed above and he will harvest the following blessings.

FIRST JEWEL: A harvest of righteousness, James 3:18. Righteousness means, *the doing or being what is just and right; the character and acts of a man commanded by and approved of God"*. Righteousness is something God bestows upon people who have faith, Romans 4:3. James says those with godly wisdom will reap *"a harvest of righteousness that is sown in peace by those who make peace."*

Paul wrote, *"Do not be deceived: God is not mocked, for whatever one sows, that will he also reap. For the one who sows to his own flesh will from the flesh reap corruption, but the one who sows to the Spirit will from the Spirit reap eternal life,"* Galatians 6:7-8. That sums wisdom up quite nicely doesn't it? The seeds of wisdom that we sow will certainly bear fruit that is worth harvesting.

SECOND JEWEL: A harvest sown in peace, James 3:18. Perhaps this is a reference to the Sermon on the Mount where Jesus said, *"Blessed are the peacemakers, for they shall be called 'sons' of God,"* Matthew 5:9. The wisdom that comes from God promotes peace whereas the wisdom from the world promotes disorder and every vile practice.

What is peace? The definition from the Greek lexicon is, *"peace, rest; in contrast with strife, and denoting the absence or end of strife"*. Many years ago I learned an explanation of godly peace that is very helpful to me. I do not remember where I learned it. It demonstrates the peace of God as having three parts. To have peace is: 1) To have peace with God, 2) To have peace with your fellowman, and 3) To be at peace with your self. This kind of peace allows a person to be at peace while suffering sickness, false imprisonment, and any type of tragic circumstance that might come along. Jesus left us this kind of peace, *"My peace I give to you. Not as the world gives do I give to you,"* John 14:27.

Even though we have spent an entire paragraph defining peace, the truth is, godly peace cannot be fully defined. The Christian receives, *"the peace of God that passes all understanding"*. This peace *"will guard your hearts and your minds in Christ Jesus,"* Philippians 4:7. When we produce the attributes listed in James 3:17, our lives will surely produce *"a harvest of righteousness . . . sown in peace by those who make peace."* When that happens we can better serve Jesus, the Prince of Peace.

DISCUSSION QUESTIONS:

1. List the different groups of wise men in this chapter and discuss some of their duties and qualifications.

2. Answer the question, *Who is wise and understanding among you?* Discuss ways we can identify such a person.

3. Read 1 Corinthians 1:18-31 and discuss what this passage reveals about worldly wisdom.

4. List the nine characteristics of worldly wisdom from James chapter three. Discuss what each means.

5. List the eight characteristics of the wisdom from above, James 3:17-18 and discuss their meanings.

6. Explain James 3:18.

Chapter 10

FIGHTING AND WARS AMONG YOU
James 4:1-12
James 4:1-3

"What causes quarrels and what causes fights among you? Is it not this, that your passions are at war within you? ² You desire and do not have, so you murder. You covet and cannot obtain, so you fight and quarrel. You do not have, because you do not ask. ³ You ask and do not receive, because you ask wrongly, to spend it on your passions."

This section addresses improper conduct by some within the Christian community. It is sad when some people who profess faith in Christ Jesus do not present the type of love and harmony in their daily lives that would cause other people to realize that they were children of God. Why is it when problems come between us as brethren so many of us act like people who do not know God?

That origin of such difficulties is addressed in James 4:1-3. This section begins with the question *"What causes quarrels and what causes fights among you?"* The answer is: they come from *"your passions* (that) *are at war within you".* The quarrels and fights among us come from improper behavior. Perhaps these traits are left over attitudes that were embedded in the minds of those Christians long before they obeyed the Lord. For sure, it takes time for new Christians to ferret out the old worldly mind of the past and replace it with the mind of Christ.

FIRST JEWEL: Definitions. Our first task is to define some of the words used in James 4:1-3 that describe the characteristics of the combatants involved in waging war. Remember, this war is being waged among Christians and it is being waged in an ungodly way.

Quarrels: *"To fight as in a war or battle, to strive, contend, quarrel."* This word is a battle term. The devil doesn't mind if we meet together as Christians so long as we spend our time quarrelling and fighting among ourselves. It is without question that disagreements will come. What we need to learn is how to solve our differences without destroying our relationship with each other and without causing some of our members to lose their faith.

Read Acts 6:1-7 to see how a problem in Jerusalem was handled in a godly way rather than by quarrelling and fighting. Some Grecian widows were being neglected in the daily distribution of food. Obviously some brethren were unhappy over the situation. Rather than fight and quarrel the church solved the problem in a godly manner. They appointed seven men to take care of the needs of the neglected women. The result was harmony and a renewed emphasis upon spreading the Gospel of Christ. *"And the number of the disciples multiplied greatly in Jerusalem,"* Acts 6:7.

Fights: *"To wage war."* We are not talking about a minor disagreement or argument. We are talking about a disagreement that has escalated into a war between brethren. We need to be busy fighting our spiritual battle against the devil rather than becoming distracted and waging war among ourselves. Jesus said, *"Every kingdom divided against itself is laid waste, and no city or house divided against itself will stand,"* Matthew 12:25.

Passions: *"It is used exclusively of sinful desire, which corresponds to man's depraved nature. Inward passion."* The King James Version of the Bible translates this word as *"lust"*. Solomon wrote, *"Keep your heart with all vigilance, for from it flow the springs of life,"* Proverbs 4:23. The fruit of unchecked passion is quarrelling and fighting among brethren.

Desire: *"Enjoyment, gratification,."* This word brings to mind the idea of self-gratification. Mankind has always struggled with the problem of pleasing self rather than others. God wants us to enjoy life but He wants us to do so in a godly manner. We need to realize that we are in a serious life or death struggle between the forces of good and evil, Ephesians 6:12. We should not waste our energy fighting among ourselves.

Can you see the struggle? We all want to do the right thing or we would not have become a child of God in the first place. However, we often struggle to do the good we know we need to do. I am sure we have all been there. Read Romans 7:7-25 to be reminded of just how difficult it is to do the right thing. Many times we cannot do what we know is right because of the evil desires within us. In Romans 7:19 Paul wrote, *"For I do not do the good I want, but the evil I do not want is what I keep on doing."* Our worldly desires are often a large part of the reason for our failures. Can you relate to that problem? I certainly can!

Murder: *"To take up, and carry off; of men, to kill."* The Apostle John wrote, *"Everyone who hates his brother is a murderer and you know that no murderer has eternal life abiding in him,"* 1 John 3:15. No doubt hatred is a killer. It is in direct opposition to the second greatest commandment: *"Love you neighbor as yourself"*, Matthew 22:32-40. If a person exhibits the characteristics defined in James 4:2, he could very well end up murdering (spiritually) his brother in Christ.

Covet: James 4:2. The word translated *"covet"* in this passage means, *"To have zeal for, i.e. or against any person or thing; to be zealous towards in a good or bad sense."* This is not the word compared to idolatry in Colossians 3:5. This word can be translated by the English word *"zeal"*. It is translated *"desire"* in 1 Corinthians 14:1 when the text says, *"earnestly desire the spiritual gifts"*. James said, *"You covet (zealously long for in a wrong way) and cannot obtain, so you fight and quarrel,"* James 4:2. Zeal is a wonderful attribute when properly directed. Otherwise, it can become very divisive and destructive.

All of the words we just studied are descriptive words describing improper conduct. These verses speak of spiritual misconduct not of physical fights. They were having a war of words. It does not mean they were literally murdering people but they were killing the faith of some. He is speaking of improper passion that produces improper actions between brothers and sisters in Christ. The problem began with misguided passions and ended up as a war with many casualties.

SECOND JEWEL: Disaster strikes. When God's people do not demonstrate the wisdom from above they go to war. When that happens they suffer casualties and many spiritual disasters. I am sure you have heard of churches that have experienced such wars or perhaps you even lived through such battles. I know I have. Here are some examples of situations that could cause the church to go to war among its members.

Fighting over a minister. Rumblings of war often go up when church leaders decide it is time to change preachers. Sometimes the congregation disagrees with the decision made by the church leaders. Before long there is a full-blown war going on. If emotions are not brought under control the result will be division. I know situations where friends became enemies and churches eventually split into two congregations over the issue of changing preachers.

Sadly, when this happens, some people become so angry they lose their faith and quit the church. When our *"passions are at war within"* us the results are never good. When we don't like a leadership decision it is appropriate for us to let our feelings be known but we don't have to go to war by trying to force our will on the matter. We must face the fact that we don't have all the inside information that led the church leaders to their decision.

The role of a preacher asked to leave his pulpit duties is also important. How could a preacher move to a congregation for the purpose of building them up in the Lord and then tear them down because he was asked to leave? Even if the man didn't want to go he should leave gracefully in order to promote love and harmony among the brethren. Very likely, God has great plans in store for the preacher at another congregation. When we are seeking peace we will seek diligently to find a way not to go to war against each other.

Fighting over good works. Sometimes people go to war over pet projects. Suppose a new family moves to town from another congregation and places membership. The church they attended in another city had a very active mission program. Naturally, these new members bring with them a strong desire to promote missions in their new church home.

However, in this case, the church leaders were not ready to take on any new mission work. In their judgment the timing for taking on an expanded mission program was not right due to a lack of finances. For that reason they delayed any expansion in missions to a later date. There have been cases when a refusal like this has resulted in a war between brethren. If the desire (zeal) of the new members becomes a war cry then there will be casualties of war. We need to learn to have disagreements without waging war. Solomon wrote that God hates, *"one who sows discord among brothers,"* Proverbs 6:19.

THIRD JEWEL: Handling differences of opinion. There will be times when we have differences of opinion. Wise Christians will work these things out without going to war. Notice the difference of opinion that occurred between Paul and Barnabas in Acts 15:36-41. Paul and Barnabas could not agree on the proposal to take John Mark along with them on their Second Missionary Journey. Barnabas said, *"Yes"* but Paul said, *"No"*. They could not come to a satisfactory agreement.

Therefore, they ended up going their separate ways but they departed as friends not as enemies. They were passionate but not with the evil passion James spoke about. They went their separate ways but the result was two mission teams instead of one. It turned out to be a victory not a defeat.

Later on, Paul had good things to say about Mark. He said Mark was, *"very useful to me for ministry,"* 2 Timothy 4:11. We need to strive to work out our differences in a way that glorifies God and allows us to remain friends rather engaging in quarrels and wars. To fight and win at all costs only gives the devil the victory.

PRAYER PROBLEMS
James 4:2b-3

"You do not have, because you do not ask. ³ You ask and do not receive, because you ask wrongly, to spend it on your passions."

The problems discussed in James 4:2-3 can even affect a Christians' prayer life. There are two hindrances to successful prayer discussed in these verses.

FIRST JEWEL: A failure to pray. *"You do not have, because you do not ask"*. God expects His children to talk to Him. Developing a proper prayer life is essential to one's spiritual growth. Often we get too busy to pray. Such a thing should never happen to a child of God but it does. Sometimes we all get so busy *"serving"* we fail to pray. Other times, when we are filled with worldly passions or anger we just don't have the heart to pray like we should. Quarreling often brings about anger and that can hinder our prayer life. When there is sin in our life it becomes very difficult to offer up prayers to God.

SECOND JEWEL: Praying with improper motives. *"You ask and do not receive, because you ask wrongly, to spend it on your passions"* James 4:3. This is the person who is praying but is asking for the wrong reasons. Prayer is not a *"want list"* intended to fulfill all our desires. We won't receive a positive answer if we ask God for things that are based upon worldly passions.

We will look at prayer again when we study James 5:16-18. For now just realize that if we have legitimate requests but fail to ask for them, we will not receive an answer. To get an affirmative answer to our prayers, we must ask for things according to God's will, 1 John 5:14-15.

The lives of the people to whom James wrote were in turmoil. Instead of the peace that passes understanding they were quarrelling and fighting. Until they changed their ways, they would never enjoy the blessings of answered prayer.

WHOSE FRIEND ARE YOU?
James 4:4-6

"You adulterous people. Do you not know that friendship with the world is enmity with God? Therefore whoever wishes to be a friend of the world makes himself an enemy of God. ⁵ Or do you suppose it is to no purpose that the Scripture says, 'He yearns jealously over the spirit that he has made to dwell in us?' ⁶ But he gives more grace. Therefore it says, "God opposes the proud, but gives grace to the humble."

This passage delivers a frightening message to the Christian. It informs us that friendship with the world is enmity *"an enemy, adversary"* with God. If we stand in opposition to God, who do you think would win?

In 1 John 2:15-17 we read a similar warning. Part of the passage reads, *"Do not love the world or the things in the world. . . . the world is passing away along with its desires, but whoever does the will of God abides forever".* As a child of God, we live in the world but we are not of the world. Remember, the world we are to hate is not the physical universe God created. We love the animals, the stars, the moon, the sun and all the beautiful things God brought forth by the power of His word. In fact, we stand in awe of our Mighty God and His creative power.

The passage in 1 John 2:15-17 commands us to hate the sinful things of the world. We are to hate the *"desires of the flesh, the desires of the eyes and the pride in possessions"*. To do any differently is to become an enemy of God Himself. I find it amazing that even good things can become evil when people carry them to extremes. For example, money is good but the love of money is *"a root of all kinds of evil"*, 1 Timothy 6:10. Dear God, please help us not to allow our worldly passions to make us your enemy!

In an ideal Christian community, those outside of Christ would marvel at the difference in conduct between the Christians and the unbelievers. They would see dedicated worshippers gathering together on the Lord's Day. They would see pure and holy conduct in every facet of life. They would see people sharing their faith on a regular basis and a long list of other attributes proving one to be a child of God. In our day and age, far too often, interested onlookers cannot see any difference between the life and actions of *"believers"* and *"unbelievers"*. My brethren, these things ought not so to be! We cannot be the light of the world if the switch is turned off!

James 4:5 is a difficult verse to understand. The ESV translates the verse as follows, *"Or do you suppose it is to no purpose that the Scripture says, "He yearns jealously over the spirit that he has made to dwell in us"?* The word jealously is often translated, *"envy"* and has the meaning *"jealous of another's success, depreciation of his worth"*. The word is usually used in a bad sense. Since God has no evil attributes that cannot be the meaning in this verse. The King James Bible translates the verse, *"Do ye think that the scripture saith in vain, The spirit that dwelleth in us lusteth to envy?"* The translation given by these two versions of the Bible are quite different.

There is no direct quotation in Scripture that matches this verse. Some scholars believe James is not quoting directly from scripture but is paraphrasing one or more Old Testament verses. Others, such as the ESV and the RSV make God the subject of the verse and consider this a loose quotation from the Song of Moses in Deuteronomy 32:16, 21.

The translation provided in the ESV version fits into the context of James quite nicely when you include James 4:6 into the mix. The Lord *"yearns jealously over the spirit that he has made to dwell in us,"* James 4:5. And *"he gives more grace. Therefore it says, 'God opposes the proud, but gives grace to the humble,'"* James 4:6. The verses seem to be saying God yearns zealously for the spirit of man, a spirit often filled with evil desires, that the person could humble himself and receive the grace of God. You might want to delve more deeply into this verse by looking at other commentaries that explain this verse.

HUMBLE YOURSELF TO GOD
James 4:7-10

"Submit yourselves therefore to God. Resist the devil, and he will flee from you. ⁸ Draw near to God, and he will draw near to you. Cleanse your hands, you sinners, and purify your hearts, you double-minded. ⁹ Be wretched and mourn and weep. Let your laughter be turned to mourning and your joy to gloom. ¹⁰ Humble yourselves before the Lord, and he will exalt you."

We have already noted how James likes to bring up important topics over and over again. He now looks at humility one more time. We begin with submission and end up with humility and exaltation.

FIRST JEWEL: Submit to God, James 4:7. This section begins with the word *"submit"*. It means, *"to put under, to subordinate, to make subject"*. Submission is to be done willingly, of our own accord. We, of our own volition, place our self under the authority of the Lord. This is the first step towards acquiring humility.

When I was in Junior High school some of my friends and I loved sneaking behind someone in order to twist his arm up behind his back. We would not turn loose until our victim cried out *"Uncle!"* This is not the type of submission God requires of His children. He wants us to follow the lead of David, and others, who submitted as the voluntary act of a penitent sinner. There was no crying *"Uncle!"* when David came before God confessing his sins. Instead, there was total submission to the God of heaven and there was the humble admission he was a sinful man.

SECOND JEWEL: Resist the devil, *"Resist the devil, and he will flee from you,"* James 4:7. After submission comes resistance. The devil is resolved to tempt us to do evil. In most cases, if we resist him he will flee from us. Of course, we must resist him with the powerful word of God. Have you noticed how Jesus fought against the temptation of the devil? He used scripture to overthrow the schemes of the devil. We can do the same thing if we know the word of God.

Once when I was in grade school, I hit a boy who was smaller and younger than me. Unknown to me, he had a big brother who attended the same school. After school, this big brother threatened to beat me up for hitting his little brother. Fortunately I lived close to school (only one block away) so I ran towards home just as fast as I could. I could hear him running behind me and was certain he was gaining ground with each step!

As I crossed into my yard, my father was in the process of mowing the lawn. I do not know why he was not at work but believe me, he was a welcome sight. I turned to my enemy and motioned to him with my hand, as if to say, *"Come on if you dare!"* Of course, he did not come because my father was there.

As weak as we are we can resist the devil. We are especially strong when we are standing with our Heavenly Father on one side and Jesus on the other. Arm yourself with the word. Stay near to your Heavenly Father. Resist the evil one and God will give you the victory!

THIRD JEWEL: Move towards God. *"Draw near to God, and he will draw near to you,"* James 4:8a. We submit, we resist, and then we move towards God. When we move towards the Lord He will come closer to us as well. Actually, the Lord is never out of our reach. He told the prophet, *"Am I a God at hand, declares the Lord and not a God afar off?" Jeremiah 23:23.* James teaches us if we make the first step (draw near unto God) the Lord will respond in kind (draw near unto us).

God is much like the father in the story of the prodigal son, Luke 15:11-32. The father stood by the roadside waiting for his *"lost"* son to return. Once the prodigal son reflected upon his sinful condition with a repentant attitude he came to the decision to return home. He began walking down the road towards home rehearsing the words he would say to his father. When his father saw him coming down the road he rushed to his son's side and commanded his servants to prepare the fatted calf. The lost son was restored to his father with joy. When we move towards Him, He will receive us **with joy.** *"Draw near to God, and he will draw near to you!"* God is like that – He really is!

FOURTH JEWEL: Get your life right with God. *"Be wretched and mourn and weep. Let your laughter be turned to mourning and your joy to gloom,"*

James 4:9. This verse instructs us to clean up our spiritual lives. We are to wash our hands and purify our hearts. Of course he is not speaking of physical cleansing. This verse suggests repentance and a changed life. This is similar in meaning to the second Beatitude, *"Blessed are those who mourn, for they shall be comforted,"* Matthew 5:4. The idea is, when we become aware of our sinfulness we become wretched, and we mourn, and we weep. There is no laughter or joy for the fallen Christian until he is once again right with God.

No doubt these verses were needed for those who were guilty of quarreling and fighting with each other. Doing so was a sin and they needed to submit, draw near, and be filled with sorrow for their sin. The result would be forgiveness and humility.

FIFTH JEWEL: The humble will be exalted. *"Humble yourselves before the Lord, and he will exalt you."* True humility, like that mentioned in this passage, will result in exaltation. And, it is God who will exalt us not we ourselves. But the Lord will exalt us at a time of His own choosing. It could be in this life or it could be in the life to come. In either case God will keep his promise. *"Humble yourself, therefore, under the mighty hand of God so that at the proper time he may exalt you,"* 1 Peter 5:6.

WE ARE NOT THE JUDGE
James 4:11-12

"Do not speak evil against one another, brothers. The one who speaks against a brother or judges his brother, speaks evil against the law and judges the law. But if you judge the law you are not a doer of the law but a judge. ¹²*There is only one lawgiver and judge, he who is able to save and to destroy. But who are you to judge your neighbor?"*

As a follow-up to humble repentance and restoration James now teaches us not to speak evil against one another. Imagine this scene. A Christian quarrels and fights with another Christian brother. The problem is well known to the entire church. Then, in the privacy of his home, in humble submission to the Lord, the sinner expresses deep sorrow, he repents and he prays for forgiveness. Because the sin is well known to most of the congregation, the repentant brother goes before the entire congregation and asks for forgiveness.

What would you think of such a person? Would you forgive him or would you say, *"I just don't believe he is sincere."* If you spoke or thought such words then you were speaking evil against your brother. It is not our job to judge a person's sincerity. That is God's job. Aren't you glad God is the judge and not man?

FIRST JEWEL: Don't speak evil against one another. *"Do not speak evil against one another, brothers. The one who speaks against a brother or judges his brother, speaks evil against the law and judges the law. But if you judge the law you are not a doer of the law but a judge,"* James 4:11. Speaking evil against one another makes us the judge. By making ourselves the judge we are speaking evil against the law. By imposing our own will into the matter we override God's will. It makes us a judge and not a doer of the law. We would be wise to leave the judging of the heart to God.

SECOND JEWEL: God is the lawgiver and judge! *"There is only one lawgiver and judge, he who is able to save and to destroy. But who are you to judge your neighbor?"* James 4:12. Based on the teaching found in 1 Corinthians 6:1-11 we are to judge disputes and matters of civil law between brethren. We are allowed to judge these things because they involve outward actions that wise brethren can look at and make a wise judgment. They can help us solve such issues without going to a court of law.

Judging in the context of James 4:12, has to do with judging one's heart. This is quite different from judging civil disputes. We learn in John 2:25 that Jesus did not need to be told what a person was thinking because He knew what was in a man. The rest of us do not have that ability. So, be careful not to judge a person's sincerity because of an argument or quarrel. To do so speaks against the law. *"But who are you to judge your neighbor?"* Beware lest we become the judge in matters that belong to the Lord. Never forget, God is both the lawgiver and the judge!

DISCUSSION QUESTIONS:

1. According to James, what causes quarrels and fights among us?

2. Discuss James' use of the terms war, murder, and adultery. What is he talking about?

3. Discuss prayer problems as presented in James 4:2. How can we learn to offer better prayers? Search for some other scriptures that will help you improve your prayer life?

4. Discuss the problem of *"friendship with the world"* in James 4:4-6.

5. Discuss the *"jewels"* listed under the heading **HUMBLE YOURSELF TO GOD**.

6. Discuss the difference between judging the heart and judging one's actions.

Chapter 11

BOASTING ABOUT TOMORROW
A DIFFERENT LIFESTYLE
James 4:13-17

James 4:13-17

"Come now, you who say, 'Today or tomorrow we will go into such and such a town and spend a year there and trade and make a profit.' ¹⁴Yet you do not know what tomorrow will bring. What is your life? For you are a mist that appears for a little time and then vanishes. ¹⁵Instead you ought to say, 'If the Lord wills, we will live and do this or that.' ¹⁶As it is, you boast in your arrogance. All such boasting is evil. ¹⁷So whosoever knows the right thing to do and fails to do it, for him it is sin."

MAKING A LIVING

We all know the importance of making a living. The Bible clearly teaches, *"if a man is not willing to work, he should not eat"*, 2 Thessalonians 3:10. Therefore, the need to work is an important issue. Our passage, James 4:13-17, does not forbid working in order to make a living or making plans for the future. Neither is it intended to forbid a man from making a profit. Why, then, was it written and what does it mean?

The purpose is to provide us with a warning against planning our daily affairs in such a way that we leave God out of our plans. The child of God must seek God's will in all that he does. We don't just seek the will of God on Sunday when we meet to worship and then forget all about Him during the week. We must seek His will in every area of our life every hour of every day.

Men have a very limited view of the future. We may make plans for tomorrow, or next week, or next year but we do not really have the ability to make those things happen. When we leave God out of our plans we are only boasting in our arrogance. How many times have circumstances forced you to put your plans on hold or even cancel them all together? These things happen because we cannot control the future. All of our plans should be undertaken with the will of God in mind. To do otherwise is nothing short of sin.

James teaches us this important principle and then he instructs us to do the right thing. If we knowingly fail to do what we know is right, our action becomes a sin. How thankful we should be for the warnings given to us in the Holy Bible against trying to manage our lives apart from God's presence. We must always be alert to His will, a process that is enhanced through bible study. We must also talk to Him regularly in our prayers asking for wisdom and direction in our lives. Study and prayer gives us a much better chance for success as we plan the strategies we want to use for directing our lives.

WORK IS A BLESSING FROM GOD
James 4:13

"Come now, you who say, 'Today or tomorrow we will go into such and such a town and spend a year there and trade and make a profit.'"

Working for a living has always been an absolute necessity. When you look at Adam and Eve in the Garden of Eden you learn that God gave them work to do from the very beginning. Some mistakenly believe work was the curse placed upon Adam because of his sin but that is not true. Genesis 2:15 says, *"The LORD God took the man and put him in the Garden of Eden to work it and keep it"*. Thus Adam was given a job to do before he and Eve even thought about eating fruit from the forbidden tree.

After Adam and Eve sinned in the Garden of Eden, their work became much more difficult. Because of their sin, God cursed the ground so that it brought forth thorns and thistles. From Adam onward, mankind has had to eat his bread by the sweat of his brow. I have noticed that weeds, dandelions, and other pesky things like crab grass, grow faster and with less water than the good stuff. In fact you don't even have to tend these things for them to grow. I have often threatened (with tongue in cheek) to plant weeds in my flower garden because they would prosper and grow without my help. Work was not the curse given to Adam and Eve. It was the ground God cursed not working for a living.

The problem with the people in James 4:13 was not that they planned to work in a certain town in order to establish a business. It was not that they wanted to stay for a specific length of time and make a profit. Their problem was making plans for their lives without considering the will of the Lord. Quite simply, they were leaving God out of their plans.

THE LIMITATIONS OF MAN
James 4:14-16

"Yet you do not know what tomorrow will bring. What is your life? For you are a mist that appears for a little time and then vanishes. ¹⁵Instead you ought to say, 'If the Lord will, we will live and do this or that.' ¹⁶As it is, you boast in your arrogance. All such boasting is evil."

God does not want us to live our lives using our own power and wisdom. Our Heavenly Father wants us to live under the umbrella of His Divine will. There are steps we can take to assist us in finding it. Most of us really do want to know and do His will. Right? Of course we do. Sometimes it is just not that easy for us to determine His will.

FIRST JEWEL: We don't know the future. *"Yet you do not know what tomorrow will bring,"* James 4:14. It has already been mentioned that we have a limited view of the future. That, in and of itself, is enough of a reason to cause a person to seek help from the One who holds the future in His hands. The prophets were able to reveal future events because of knowledge given them by an all-knowing God. The rest of us cannot foretell future events with any measure of accuracy.

One day, an elder in the church where I served came to see me on a Saturday morning. The two of us discussed projects and plans for the church. It was a lovely and meaningful discussion. When he left he told me, *"I have to go home and mow the grass. The Lord willing, I'll see you tomorrow"*. Two hours later I received a phone call that this beloved brother had dropped dead while mowing his grass. We just don't know the future.

His words are burned into my memory. *"The Lord willing, I'll see you tomorrow."* Solomon wrote, *"The living know they will die"*, Ecclesiastes 9:5. We just don't know when that day will come. While it is admirable to make plans for the future, we must be sure to include the idea, *"If the Lord wills, we will live and do this or that".* My friend, Floyd, provided me with a great example of seeking the Lord's will when he spoke his last words to me on that fateful Saturday morning. *"The Lord willing, I'll see you tomorrow."*

SECOND JEWEL: Life is short. *"What is your life? For you are a mist that appears for a little time and then vanishes,"* James 4:14. Wouldn't it be nice to have a direct line to heaven where we could call the Lord and ask Him what day we were going to die? I suppose some people would be a bit more prepared if they had that knowledge. The correct attitude is to live every day as if it was your last day to live.

THIRD JEWEL: Seek His will in all you do. *"Instead you ought to say, 'If the Lord wills, we will live and do this or that.' As it is, you boast in your arrogance. All such boasting is evil,"* James 4:15-16. We have learned we have limited knowledge of the future. What about the present? What is His will for us today? Smart phones have many great capabilities but they don't go quite that far do they?

Truthfully, it is often very difficult to determine the will of God for our lives. When Jesus faced His death on the cross He asked God to deliver Him from the cup that was before Him. Here is what our Lord said. *"My Father, if it be possible, let this cup pass from me; nevertheless, not as I will, but as you will,"* Matthew 26:39. Doing the will of God was not easy for Jesus either. However, even though He asked for deliverance, Jesus fully intended to submit to His Father's will to the very end.

FOURTH JEWEL: Failure to do what you know is right is a sin. To leave God out of our plans is *"boastful arrogance. All such boasting is evil."* This passage closes with very sobering words. *"So whosoever knows the right thing to do and fails to do it, for him it is sin,"* James 4:17. The conclusion of this scripture warns us that a failure to seek the will of the Lord is a sin. Sounds like something extremely important to me!

A SPECIAL STUDY
FINDING THE WILL OF GOD

As we begin this special study we want to establish two areas of life where we need to find God's will. The first one deals with the decisions we make in our day-to-day life. The second has to do with decisions that govern our spiritual life. Even though there are two areas to consider, do not make the mistake of trying to separate the two. If God cannot have all of us, He will take nothing. We need God's help in making decisions that affect both our physical and our spiritual life. They are a bit different but both are of vital importance.

When it comes to finding the will of God, it is not as if He is going to email us with instructions nor will He speak to us in the middle of the night. It is often a difficult task to determine what the Lord would have us to do. Over the years I have come up with some ideas on the topic that are helpful to me. Hopefully they will be of value to you too.

MAKING DAY-TO-DAY DECISIONS

To me, these are the most difficult we have to make. That is because much of the time there is no specific commandment from God to help us determine His will. For example, what occupation should I pursue? Where should I live, what kind of house should I purchase? Should I buy a new car? The list of questions and the need to make a good decision goes on and on every single day of our life. How do we decide such things? These are the kind of decisions touched upon in James 4:13-17. Since there is no *"Thus says the Lord"* for these decisions we must find the answer elsewhere.

In making day-to-day decisions we need to recognize our own limitations. Jeremiah wrote, *"I know, O LORD, that the way of man is not in himself, that it is not in man who walks to direct his steps,"* Jeremiah 10:23. Wise men from the past recognized their own limitations and as a consequence sought help from Jehovah God. How much more should we, who have the Gospel of Christ, depend upon Him to lead us towards His precious will? Below are some helpful questions to ask yourself when you are searching for God's will.

QUESTIONS TO ASK YOURSELF

1. Have I prayed to God for wisdom to make a decision that is fully in accord with His will?
2. Have I searched the scriptures to see if there is a direct command or principle that would have a bearing upon the decision I want to make?
3. Will making this decision have a negative impact upon my relationship to either God or my family?
4. Have I asked my mate, my family, or a trusted friend their opinion?
5. Will this decision diminish my ability to serve the Lord? This has to do with time and space. Will I be too busy? Will I have to travel too far? These and other issues need to be addressed before making your decision.
6. Will purchasing a car, or house or any other expensive item, impact my ability to give as generously to the Lord as He would have me to do? God wants us to give as we have prospered so the work of the Lord can be accomplished. If I have a full budget and purchase a new car anyway, how will it affect my ability to contribute to the Lord? Something will need to be adjusted. If the only way you can purchase a big-ticket item is to decrease or eliminate your contribution to the Lord, then it is the wrong decision.
7. Does the new job involve ethics, procedures, or products that are questionable for a Christian to do?

Taking enough time to think things through, spending time in prayer, and fully considering how your decision will impact your spiritual life will help you find the will of God.

If you cannot determine for sure just what you should do, you will have to make the best decision you can make knowing that *"all things work together for good, for those who are called according to his purpose,"* Romans 8:28. Sometimes it will become obvious your decision was not a good one. In that case, do what needs to be done to correct your error. Other times, there could be more than one good choice for you to choose from. While one decision might be better than another, it may not matter which choice you make. Just do your best and let God work it out for your good.

MAKING SPIRITUAL DECISIONS

Finding the spiritual based decision is easier to find than the day-to-day decisions of life because we can turn to the Bible for answers. That is especially true when it comes to God's commandments. Finding a passage that deals with the issue at hand will settle the issue for those who believe in Him. Even so, it is still difficult and we sometimes make wrong choices. If that becomes apparent, then get some help from a learned spiritual leader on how to overcome a wrong decision.

BELIEVE GOD HAS A PURPOSE FOR YOUR LIFE: *"For I know the plans I have for you, declares the LORD, plans for wholeness and not for evil, to give you a future and a hope,"* Jeremiah 29:11. We know this passage was written for the Jewish people living in Babylonian exile and was a promise for their future return to Judah. However, why would we think God has plans for them and has no plans for us? Give yourself over to Him and He will care for you.

DO NOT LIMIT GOD: *"Now to him who is able to do far more abundantly than all that we ask or think, according to the power at work within us, to Him be glory in the church and in Christ Jesus throughout all generations, forever and ever. Amen,"* Ephesians 3:20-21. This great passage informs us of the super abundant power God has to bless His people when we place our requests before Him in prayer. Look at the wording of this passage. The Lord can *"do far more abundantly than all that we ask or think"*. Tie this verse in with 1 John 2:14-15 and we learn that blessings come as we ask for the things that are according to His will. Answered prayers reveal to us the will of God.

STRIVE TO KNOW GOD'S WILL FOR YOUR LIFE: *"Therefore do not be foolish, but understand what the will of the Lord is,"* 1 Thessalonians 5:17. The Apostle Paul calls the failure to know the will of the Lord foolishness. The Greek word translated *"foolish"* means, *"without mind, simple, ignorant"*. Don't be mindless and ignorant; learn the will of God for your life. This is accomplished by a diligent and thorough study of the word of God. The Bible contains His will.

GOD'S WILL AND SIN: Some decisions are much easier to determine than others. For example, we know God does not want us to continue our sin. The Lord's will is that we do not sin. *"My little children, I am writing these things to you so that you may not sin,"* 1 John 2:1. However, all of us

DO sin even though our goal is not to do so.

How do we accomplish this task? We must learn what is sinful and what is not. David wrote, *"I have stored up your word in my heart, that I might not sin against you,"* Psalm 119:11. Later in this same Psalm David listed the benefits of Bible knowledge. Some of those benefits were wisdom, understanding, more knowledge than his teachers and the aged, his feet were kept from every evil way, and he had an ability not to turn aside from God's rules. This knowledge caused David to hate every false way, Psalm 119:97-104. No wonder David said, *"How sweet are your words to my taste, sweeter than honey to my mouth".* Knowing the word of God will help you find His will and help you not to sin.

GOD'S WILL AND WORSHIP: It is God's will for us *"to worship Him in spirit and in truth"*, John 4:24. We are not to neglect the assembling of ourselves together, Hebrews 10:25. The example of the early Christians was to meet frequently. At first, they seemed to meet everyday, Acts 2:46. Far too many people today are looking for ways to worship less and less rather than more and more. What is God's will on this matter?

Some believers make a decision not to worship on Sunday based upon how they feel, or whether it is a good day for fishing, or whether they are in the mood to worship. Someone says, *"I just can't worship today, I am too tired."* or *"I am too depressed to go anywhere today!"* Others say, *"My friends are in town for a visit so I can't go to worship today."* What do you think the will of God is on this matter? Where would He have you to be on the Lord's Day?

My suggestion is that believers make the decision to be in worship every single time the saint's meet. That means on Sunday morning or Sunday evening, or Wednesday, or for special lectureships and meetings. Why not make the decision right now, today, and then make it a permanent part of your life. It sure will make life easier for you. When Sunday morning arrives you will know immediately that you will be going to worship the Lord. Do you think that is His will for you?

GOD'S WILL AND HOLINESS: There is no doubt that God said, *"You shall be holy, for I am holy,"* 1 Peter 2:16. To carry out God's will in this matter, we need to learn what holiness is and learn how to make it a part of our Christian character. We are made holy through the blood of Jesus

Christ. We remain holy by living a holy lifestyle. The word of God will teach us how to live a holy life.

Finding God's will for our lives on many topics is ours for the asking. All we have to do is study the word and we will be able to learn the commandments of the Lord. Then, all we have to do is to keep them. *"For this is the love of God, that we keep his commandments. And his commandments are not burdensome,"* 1 John 5:4. Like the sweet psalmist of Israel said, *"Your word is a lamp to my feet and a light to my path,"* Psalm 119:105. When we seek to know the will of God for our lives we will find it, Matthew 7:7-8. After all, God would not expect us to do His will if it were impossible for us to find it.

GOING TO THAILAND

Just before my graduation from the Sunset International Bible Institute, Parker Henderson, a longtime missionary to Thailand, invited us to join a team of ten families picked to serve as missionaries to the country of Thailand. Once I was convinced this was where we should go, I set out to find churches and individuals willing to support us in our chosen field. Of course, many prayers went up to the Lord. We were excited and eager to get ready for our move to Bangkok. Weeks and months passed and we still did not have the support we needed. When things became critical, financially speaking, we were forced to change our plans. Thankfully, a church that had agreed to support us in Asia asked me to serve as their pulpit minister. We accepted. I, for one, was very disappointed that we had to scrap our plans to join the Thailand team.

Less than two years later my wife and I attended a lectureship at Abilene Christian University. Many speakers emphasized reaching a lost and dying world with the Gospel. My heart was touched deeply. As we drove home we discussed our persistent desire to enter the mission field and also discussed our previous failure to secure the needed funding.

In discussing the issue I realized, for the first time, in our effort to go to Thailand two years earlier we had not sought out God's will. We just assumed He wanted us to go and that He would provide the resources necessary for us to do so. No wonder we failed! This time, we determined to commit our lives to serving in a mission field of God's own choosing. Anywhere would be just fine with us. We prayed that it would be His will for us go to a mission field somewhere and preach the gospel of Christ.

This time we would not seek to impose our will upon God. Such an approach would guarantee failure.

We arrived home just in time for me to teach my Wednesday night class. That very night, after we arrived home, my telephone rang. It was an elder from a church in Alabama. The conversation began like this, *"We understand you are a missionary wanting to go to Thailand. Well, we are a church looking for someone to send there."* We made a trip to that congregation for an interview and in just a few months we were able to join our original mission team in Bangkok, Thailand.

This story sounds like a made up story doesn't it? Yet, amazingly, it is absolutely true! Every time I read James chapter four, I am brought to my knees and I remember the need to seek God's will for all of my plans and not to try to do things by my own wisdom and power. Always keep God's will in your mind and put Him in your plans. By doing so, you will surely be successful.

DISCUSSION QUESTIONS:

1. Discuss the importance of work from the days of Adam until today.

2. Discuss the four *"jewels"* under the topic, **THE LIMITATIONS OF MAN**.

3. Discuss the two areas of our life where we seek the will of God listed in the special study, **FINDING THE WILL OF GOD**. While they are different can they be separated? If so, how? If not, why not?

4. Discuss the questions we should ask ourselves when making decisions regarding our day-to-day lives that will help us find the will of God.

5. Discuss the six ideas presented under the heading **MAKING SPIRITUAL DECISIONS**.

Chapter 12

WARNING TO THE RICH AND PATIENCE IN SUFFERING
James 5:1-12

James 5:1
"Come now, you rich, weep and howl for the miseries that are coming upon you."

ANOTHER LOOK AT THE RICH

This is a logical follow-up to the discussion about those boastful merchants who were going to go to a city for a year to buy and sell and get gain but were leaving God out of their plans. We already spoke of the rich when we studied James 2:1-11 under the topic of showing partiality. Actions of the wealthy in this section suggest they were unbelievers. If they were Christians they were in dire need of repentance.

We have already noticed how James likes to introduce a subject, discuss it a bit, and then introduce a new topic? Later on he will go back and give more details on the subject previously introduced.

TOPIC	PASSAGES IN JAMES
The Rich	1:10; 2:2-6; 5:1-6
Works	1:22, 26-27; 2:14-26; 3:13
The Tongue	1:26; 3:1-12
Wisdom	1:5-8; 3:13-18
Trials and Suffering	1:2-4; 12-15; 5:7-11; 13

Generally speaking the rich are not only privileged by their wealth and status in the community but they are often honored simply because of the wealth they have acquired. God looks at things differently than men. He warns the rich to change their ways or they will suffer dire consequences.

The Bible tells us about rich men of faith who were not corrupted by their wealth. Abraham, Job, and King David are just a few examples of extremely rich men who did not abuse the wealth God gave them. One of the problems for the rich is the tendency to trust in their riches rather than to trust in the One who blessed them with their wealth.

THE DIFFICULTY OF CONVERTING THE RICH

Jesus met a rich young ruler in Matthew 19:16-22. According to other gospel accounts Jesus not only talked to the young man but He loved him. After a discussion on what was needed to inherit eternal life the young ruler was told to sell all he had and give the proceeds to the poor. Because he had great riches the rich young ruler went away sorrowful.

No doubt the young man loved his wealth more than he loved God. This prompted Jesus to say, *"Truly, I say to you only with difficulty will a rich person enter the kingdom of heaven. Again I tell you, it is easier for a camel to go through the eye of a needle than for a rich person to enter the kingdom of God,"* Matthew 19:23-24. This saying astonished the disciples. It prompted them to ask, *"Who then can be saved?"* Jesus revealed a powerful truth when He replied, *"With man it is impossible, but with God all things are possible,"* Matthew 19:26. Yes, there is hope of salvation for the wealthy too.

The difficulty facing the rich is also addressed in 1 Corinthians 1:26. This passage teaches us that not many noble, not many wise, not many powerful are called by the gospel message. Maybe that is because they are doing so well in life they don't feel the need for help from God or anyone else. They rely upon their own resources to save them more than trusting in the power of the Gospel of Jesus Christ.

THE RICH MEN DESCRIBED
James 5:1-6

"Come now, you rich, weep and howl for the miseries that are coming upon you. ² Your riches have rotted and your garments are moth-eaten. ³ Your gold and silver have corroded, and their corrosion will be evidence against you and will eat your flesh like fire. You have laid up treasure in the last days. ⁴ Behold, the wages of the laborers who mowed your fields, which you kept back by fraud, are crying out against you, and the cries of the harvesters have reached the ears of the

Lord of hosts. *⁵ You have lived on the earth in luxury and in self-indulgence. You have fattened your hearts in a day of slaughter. ⁶ You have condemned and murdered the righteous person. He does not resist you."*

James gives us a strange description of the rich. If we didn't know better, we would think he was addressing those who were poor and downtrodden. But, he is addressing the sorry spiritual state of those who were rich and powerful. It is clear that their deficiencies were spiritual and not physical.

FIRST JEWEL: Misused riches bring sorrow, *"Weep and howl for the miseries that are coming upon you,"* James 5:2. Generally speaking the rich can buy their way out of a bad situation. When it comes to their spiritual condition that is not true! This scripture is not saying the rich will be miserable because of their wealth. It is saying a misuse of wealth will bring much sorrow on the Day of Judgment.

SECOND JEWEL: Hoarded riches are wasteful, *"Your gold and silver have corroded, and their corrosion will be evidence against you and will eat your flesh like fire. You have laid up treasure in the last days,"* James 5:3. It is not wrong to put money back for the future and for emergencies. However, the rich in question were hoarding up the money for themselves. This abuse makes their money as useless as it would be if it were corroded!

The parable of the rich fool, Luke 12:13-21, helps us understand the folly of hoarding riches selfishly. The application of the parable is: riches hoarded up for self, with no thought for those in need, are wasted riches. God called the rich man a fool and pronounced his imminent death. *"God said to him, Fool! This night your soul is required of you and the things you have prepared, whose will they be? So is the one who lays up treasure for himself and is not rich toward God,"* Luke 12:20-21.

The godly rich are very different from the man in the parable of the rich man. Even though they might live an affluent lifestyle, the godly rich are always happy to share their resources with those in need. They strive to use their wealth to the glory of God.

THIRD JEWEL: Misused riches is evidence against the rich, *"Behold, the wages of the laborers who mowed your fields, which you kept back by fraud, are crying out against you, and the cries of the harvesters have reached the ears of the Lord of hosts. You have lived on the earth in luxury and in self-indulgence. You have fattened your hearts in a day of slaughter,"* James 5:4-5. On the Day of Judgment the abuse of one's wealth will be brought up as evidence against the wicked rich. The abuses listed by James show a severe misuse of wealth.

1. They defrauded the poor by withholding wages from them. Just know that God hears the cries of defrauded workers. God hears their cries and will take action against the evildoers. Sometimes the Lord's justice is meted out quickly and other times justice won't come until the Day of Judgment. However, you can rest assured that God will take vengeance upon those who treat others unfairly.

2. They lived in luxury and self-indulgence while, at the very same time, they were cheating workers in the field. Their inconsistency showed a heart that failed to feel any responsibility to care for those workers who toiled so diligently to make them rich. The words of Jesus speak to sinful rich men. *"What will it profit a man if he gains the whole world and forfeits his life?"* Matthew 16:26.

3. They lived in self-indulgence while at the same time they deprived their workers of their day's wages. It is not wrong to have things to live but it is wrong to live to have things. It is also wrong to hire workers and deprive them of their pay.

4. They murdered the righteous poor. When rich land owners deprive workers of a proper salary the workers cannot take proper care of their families. Sometimes wives or children die from malnutrition. Sometimes the workers themselves become ill and die. While the rich landowner might not kill the person with his own hands, his fraudulent practices could certainly lead to their death. Notice how the workers cried out to the Lord because of the abuses they suffered. Also notice that the Lord heard their cries!

When the rich mistreat the poor there is not a lot that can be done about it. James put it simply when he spoke of the poor. *"He does not resist you."* What could the poor do against rich landowners who refused to be just and generous? The only recourse for the poor was to call on the Lord for deliverance.

FOURTH JEWEL: Judgment will come against the wicked rich, *"You have condemned and murdered the righteous person. He does not resist you,"* James 5:6. The wealthy of whom James wrote were abusing their workers. It was not that they hated them but it was that they did not care enough.

There is somewhat of a parallel in the story of the rich man and Lazarus, Luke 16:19-31. The rich man in this story had adequate riches to care for Lazarus but did not do so. He was content to leave the scraps that fell off his table for poor Lazarus to eat. Perhaps, in some twisted way, he even pitied Lazarus. But he did not do right by the poor beggar man. Both men died. The rich man went to a place of torment while Lazarus went to Abraham's bosom. God's judgment will come upon the wicked. If not in this life, then judgment will come in the life to come.

PATIENCE IN SUFFERING
James 5:7-11

"Be patient, therefore, brothers, until the coming of the Lord. See how the farmer waits for the precious fruit of the earth, being patient about it, until it receives the early and the late rains. ⁸ You also, be patient. Establish your hearts, for the coming of the Lord is at hand. ⁹ Do not grumble against one another, brothers, so that you may not be judged; behold, the Judge is standing at the door. ¹⁰ As an example of suffering and patience, brothers, take the prophets who spoke in the name of the Lord. ¹¹ Behold, we consider those blessed who remained steadfast. You have heard of the steadfastness of Job, and you have seen the purpose of the Lord, how the Lord is compassionate and merciful."

THE COMING OF THE LORD

This section begins with a call for Christians to be patient until the coming of the Lord. There are two ideas conveyed in scripture concerning the coming of the Lord. The idea that is most understood by Christians is the second coming of Jesus at the end of time. Evidence of His coming is found in Acts 1:9-11 and in 1 Thessalonians 4:13-18, just to mention a few.

The second meaning of the *"coming of the Lord"* refers to the coming of Jesus in judgment against the wicked. Jesus has come in judgment many times since the First Century. When the Lord comes in judgment no human eye sees Him. This coming is what Jesus spoke of in Matthew 24:1-35. In this passage Jesus warned of His coming to destroy Jerusalem, an event that came to pass in 70 A.D. Speaking of that judgment, Jesus said, *"So also, when you see all these things, you know that he is near, at the very gates. Truly, I say to you, this generation will not pass away until all these things take place,"* Matthew 24:33-35. All of the generation that was alive when Jesus spoke these words has long since died. Therefore, He could not have been speaking of the end of time in Matthew 24. He was speaking of the destruction of Jerusalem in 70 A.D.

Our passage, James 5:7, spoke of the coming of the Lord in judgment against evil rich people who were mistreating their laborers. The poor were praying to the Lord for deliverance and He was hearing their prayers. Now they needed patience as they waited for the Lord's answer. They also needed to believe their prayers would soon be answered. Look at the following examples of patience.

FIRST JEWEL: Patience in harvesting, *"Be patient, therefore, brothers, until the coming of the Lord. See how the farmer waits for the precious fruit of the earth, being patient about it, until it receives the early and the late rains,"* James 5:7. In order to survive difficult circumstances we must develop patience. In the context, patience is required by those being mistreated by the rich landowners who were depriving them of proper compensation for their labor.

The key to finding peace of mind in the midst of turmoil is patience. The Greek text of the New Testament says, *"to be long-suffering, to be patiently forbearing"*. In the margin of the ESV bible there is the following explanation of the word, *"long patient"*, or *"suffer with long patience"*. When problems come in life it is not always easy to be patient as we wait on the Lord. Most of us want an immediate answer. We are much like the child who prayed, *"Lord, give me patience and give it to me right now!"*

The book of James gives us an example from the patience of a farmer. He plants and patiently waits for the harvest time to come. In Palestine there were two rainy seasons around which the planting and harvest depended. The early rains came in October and the later rains came in March. In between the farmer could water the crop, put fertilizer on the plants, pull the weeds, and protect the crop from harmful insects or animals. He could not rush the harvest. It is required that the farmer be patient.

SECOND JEWEL: Establish your hearts, *"Be patient. Establish your hearts, for the coming of the Lord is at hand,"* James 5:8. So, when troubles befall us, we pray to the Lord to help us and then we wait with patience for His answer. Before we can be patient, we must establish our hearts in faith that God hears us and will provide His deliverance. We must firmly believe that in due time an answer will come.

To establish our heart indicates something that is firmly fixed or steadfast. *"For I know whom I have believed, and I am convinced that he is able to guard until that Day what has been entrusted to me"*, 2 Timothy 1:12. If you know Him you can wait patiently for His deliverance. You are also sure that He is in charge even when things go wrong. For, *"God is faithful, and he will not let you be tempted beyond your ability, but with the temptation he will also provide the way of escape, that you may be able to endure it"*, 1 Corinthians 10:13. The two verses just listed reveal to us the steadfast patience of those who have established their hearts firmly in the God of heaven. So, come what may, we trust that He knows our situation. We believe that He hears our requests, and we patiently wait for His answer.

As we wait for an answer, we must exhibit the same kind of patience shown by a farmer nurturing a crop until harvest time. We must believe God's word that says, *"For the coming of the Lord is at hand."* This phrase means near. It is not logical to think the coming of the Lord spoken of by James refers to the end of time and the second coming of Christ. Such an interpretation would do little to comfort the poor who were being mistreated.

THIRD JEWEL: Do not grumble, *"You also, do not grumble against one another, brothers, so that you may not be judged; behold, the Judge is standing at the door,"* James 5:9. As the poor wait for Him to come, they are warned against grumbling against one another because of their circumstances. I always admire people who endure the difficulties of life and, all the while, display a total trust in God. As they suffer they patiently wait for His blessing. They

129

do not grumble or lay blame upon God for delaying nor do they blame those around them. They just wait for the Judge to pronounce sentence against the wicked.

FOURTH JEWEL: Patience from the Prophets and from Job, *"As an example of suffering and patience, brothers, take the prophets who spoke in the name of the Lord. Behold, we consider those blessed who remained steadfast. You have heard of the steadfastness of Job, and you have seen the purpose of the Lord, how the Lord is compassionate and merciful,"* James 5:10-11. What better example could be given than that of the prophets? These men of faith were God's spokesmen during the days when Israel was acting in a very sinful way. They were not appreciated when they declared, *"Thus says the LORD".* Thousands of Old Testament verses show the prophets delivering God given messages under duress and many difficulties. The words they spoke were not their own but were God's words.

The Hebrew writer puts the suffering of the prophets into perspective when he wrote of them in Hebrews 11:32-40. The later portion of that passage says, *"Some were tortured, refusing to accept release, so that they might rise again to a better life. Others suffered mocking and flogging, and even chains and imprisonment. They were stoned, they were sawn in two, they were killed with the sword. They went about in skins of sheep and goats, destitute, afflicted, mistreated – of whom the world was not worthy".* They endured such treatment because they had a strong faith that God would keep His promises. They knew even if they suffered a painful death, God would be with them. How much more should we, who have received the promises they prophesied, endure hardships and even death for the cause of Jesus? We can learn from the patience of the prophets.

The final example is that of the patriarch Job. He is mentioned as one who endured suffering through the loss of his material blessings, the children he loved, and the good heath he treasured. He did not know why he suffered and, at first, he thought God had made a mistake. The trials of Job occurred in order to prove to satan that Job, a mere mortal, had unswerving faith in the Lord his God. In the end, Jehovah God blessed Job with double blessings.

Hence James says, you have, *"seen the purpose of the Lord, how the Lord is compassionate and merciful".* What an example of patience and trust Job provides for all people who suffer through serious difficulties. Like Job we must remain steadfast in our faith. We must believe that, in the end, God will make it right.

SWEARING NOT ALLOWED!
James 5:12

"But above all, my brothers, do not swear, either by heaven or by earth or by any other oath, but let your 'yes' be yes and your 'no' be no, so that you may not fall under condemnation."

This section of scripture provides us with some very important information against swearing or taking oaths. The beginning of this verse seems to refer to the Sermon on the Mount, Matthew 5:33-37. Jesus warned against swearing falsely. He also warned us not to take an oath but to merely say *"yes"* or *"no"* instead. The injunction against swearing is not speaking about using profanity; it is talking about taking an oath that you will perform certain actions.

This author does not believe the teaching in either Matthew or James forbids us from taking civil and religious oaths. Some oaths are permitted. Jesus' response to the Jews during his trial constituted an oath. The Jewish officials commanded Jesus, *"I adjure you by the living God, tell us if you are the Christ, the Son of God. Jesus said to him, 'you have said so,'"* Matthew 26:63.

This is an example of taking an oath (or swearing) in response to civil authorities. The word *"adjure"* means, *"to cause to swear, to lay under the obligation of an oath"*. Many Christians still prefer to respond to a court of law *"I affirm to tell the truth"* rather than to *"swear to tell the truth"*. Study it for yourself and make up your own mind.

To swear or take an oath that we will do something in our daily affairs is not something we should do. Both Jesus and James give this restriction. After all, circumstances could arise that would prevent us from keeping our oath. If we swear (take an oath or vow) and do not do what we promised, we will be condemned. *"Be not rash with your mouth, nor let your heart be hasty to utter a word before God for God is in heaven and you are on earth. Therefore let your words be few. . . When you vow a vow to God, do not delay paying it, for he has no pleasure in fools. Pay what you vow. It is better that you should not vow than that you should vow and not pay,"* Ecclesiastes 5:2-5. Swearing improperly could bring us under the condemnation of the Lord. A Christian is a person who keeps his word. Therefore, a simple yes or no is sufficient. Going beyond that is to fall under the condemnation of the Lord, James 5:12.

This chapter has provided us with many important lessons that make our time on earth more meaningful. We have studied the wicked rich and how they mistreated the poor. We have looked at the need for patience as we wait for the coming of the Lord (for our deliverance). We have been given the example of the prophets and Job to assist us as we patiently wait. We have been warned against swearing. This chapter is full of wonderful lessons for us to learn.

DISCUSSION QUESTIONS:

1. Discuss the difficulty of converting the rich. Talk about the rich young ruler.

2. Discuss the four *"jewels"* concerning the misuse of riches in James 5:1-6.

3. In what ways is the term *"the coming of the Lord"* used in scripture? Give passage for proof of your answer.

4. Discuss the given *"jewels"* from James 5:8-9.

5. Discuss swearing and giving oaths. Is there any kind of swearing that is acceptable in God's sight?

Chapter 13

THE POWER OF PRAYER
James 5:13-20

James 5:13-16

"Is anyone among you suffering? Let him pray. Is anyone cheerful? Let him sing praise. ^{14} Is anyone among you sick? Let him call for the elders of the church, and let them pray over him, anointing him with oil in the name of the Lord. ^{15} And the prayer of faith will save the one who is sick, and the Lord will raise him up. And if he has committed sins, he will be forgiven. ^{16} Therefore, confess your sins to one another and pray for one another, that you may be healed. The prayer of a righteous person has great power as it is working."

PRAYER IS A WAY OF LIFE

This final chapter strengthens our understanding of the power of prayer. We all know how important prayer is but, sadly, many of us do not pray often enough or with enough fervor. Even as I write this chapter I feel the need to pray more often and to include more people and projects into my prayers. We also need to pray for those who have not yet obeyed the gospel of Jesus Christ.

We have all read the verse *"pray without ceasing,"* 1 Thessalonians 5:17. The idea is for us to begin our day with prayer, continue on during the day, and then pray once more before we go to bed at night. Prayer is a vital part of the life of a Christian. When a person gets too busy to pray, he is just too busy. Our Lord was such a man of prayer that His disciples once requested, *"Lord teach us to pray, as John taught his disciples,"* Luke 11:1. Wouldn't you love to have to have been present when Jesus taught the disciples that lesson? Actually, you can, just read Luke 11:1-13. It might not hurt to read Matthew 6:9-13 and 1 Timothy 2:1-8 as well.

PRAYERS OF SUPPLICATION AND JOY

James 5:13-17 does not teach us everything we need to know about prayer. It is limited to four areas of prayer. Most of the examples found in this passage have to do with the type of prayers that are called supplications. That means prayers that are offered on behalf of our selves or on behalf of others. The only exception in this passage has to do with times we are cheerful. In that case we sing praises to God. Here is what James teaches on the topic of prayer.

FIRST JEWEL: Pray for those who suffer. *"Is anyone among you suffering? Let him pray,"* James 5:13. The source of suffering could be illness, persecution, insensitive associates, family problems, or persecution. Whatever the source, we need to offer prayers to the Lord during difficult situations. Notice that the person who is suffering should lift up his own problems to God in prayer. From 1 Timothy 2:1, we learn that we are to pray for those who suffer as well.

SECOND JEWEL: Sing when you are happy. *"Is anyone cheerful? Let him sing praise,"* James 5:13. Being found in this list suggests that singing is but another way to offer prayers unto the Lord. For sure, many songs are prayers. Whatever the reason, the Holy Spirit placed singing in our list. It is the natural expression of a Christian's joy to lift up his voice in song.

The first time I attended a huge gathering of God's people for a lectureship in Abilene, Texas, there were over 8,000 in attendance. When the singing began, I was so overwhelmed by the sound of so many voices singing praise to the Lord that all I could do was wipe tears of joy out of my eyes. I did sing on the next song. This experience was so awe inspiring that whenever I think of it my heart still fills with pure joy of the Lord. When we are happy we sing praises!

THIRD JEWEL: Pray for the sick. *"Is anyone among you sick? Let him call for the elders of the church, and let them pray over him, anointing him with oil in the name of the Lord. And the prayer of faith will save the one who is sick, and the Lord will raise him up. And if he has committed sins, he will be forgiven,"* James 5:14-15. This passage gives us insight into the duties of church leaders. Elders are to know their flock and be sensitive to their needs. Those who are ill among us are to call for the elders of the church when they are sick. Good church leaders will quickly respond to these requests.

I remember an occasion when a church member was sick and didn't tell anyone about it until he was well. Then, he told everyone how sick he had been; readily pointing how not a single elder visited him during his illness. An understanding of James 5:14 will alleviate this problem. This passage instructs the sick to *"call for the elders of the church"*. Very simple solution isn't it? You get sick, you call for the elders, and they come to minister to your needs.

Do not overlook your personal responsibility to let the elders know you are ill. When you do, there will likely be a positive response to your needs. Both the visit and the prayer serve to encourage the sick person as well as to help them to heal. Should they need a physician or medication, that need should be provided as well.

FOURTH JEWEL: Heal the sick. *"Let them pray over him anointing him with oil in the name of the Lord. And the prayer of faith will save the one who is sick, and the Lord will raise him up,"* James 5:14b-15. Prayer is the first step towards healing. We believe that God has the power to heal the sick and that he often does so in direct response to our prayers. That is not to say that everyone we pray for will be miraculously healed. Obviously, that will not happen. The healing comes directly from the Lord in response to the prayers of the saints. God will heal whom He will. However, it is nice to know that our prayers can be the catalyst that causes the Lord to heal someone.

The second step is to anoint the sick with oil. There are two ideas put forward to explain the purpose of this anointing. Some believe the anointing with oil resulted in a miraculous healing. There were healings that took place by the laying on of hands during the First Century. Jesus and His Apostles could heal in this manner and so could other men upon whom the Apostles laid their hands. See Acts 6:1-7 for an example of men receiving the power to heal by the laying on of hands. Some believe there was such a thing as healing oil as well. That is one explanation for this verse of scripture.

This author does not believe the above explanation is correct. James speaks of anointing with oil for a purpose other than to create a miracle. Oil was used for several reasons in the Bible. First, anointing with oil was used to ordain Priests, Leviticus 8:12-13, and to ordain Kings, 1 Samuel

10:1. During the First Century oil was used in a very practical way. Women used it as a means to make their skin glossy and beautiful. Oil was used as protection from the sun. Oil was also used for medicinal purposes. This is the most likely explanation of this passage. When church leaders anointed the sick with oil they were applying a medication procedure to enhance the healing process.

Therefore, we learn that the church leaders ministered to the sick in three ways. 1) They prayed for the sick. This invokes God to intervene and heal them. 2) They anointed the sick with oil in the name of the Lord. This was to provide needed medical treatment to the sick. 3) They bring those with sin in their lives to repentance. This last point is our next discussion point.

FIFTH JEWEL: Healing the soul. *"And if he has committed sins, he will be forgiven. Therefore, confess your sins to one another and pray for one another, that you may be healed,"* James 5:15b-16a. It is important for us to realize that the health of our soul is of far more importance than the health of our bodies. Yes, the church leaders in this passage were genuinely concerned over healing the physical body. However, the visit would not have been complete if they didn't also deal with the sickness of the soul. Often a person needs to be healed in both body and soul.

Sins are forgiven when a person confesses his wrongdoing and prays for forgiveness. Far too many people are too proud to say, *"I have sinned"*. Sensitive church leaders know their flock and can discuss one's spiritual condition in such a way that the person can be saved from his sin. The leaders do not forgive sin; that is God's job. The leaders only lead sinners towards spiritual recovery. Of course, we do forgive each other, *"even as God in Christ forgave you,"* Ephesians 4:32, but the ability to remove sin is only accomplished by the Lord Himself.

We should be transparent enough to admit our sins, especially to church leaders who love us and have taken on the responsibility for our spiritual welfare. Following this teaching will help more people to be healthy in both body and soul. Nothing is better than *"double healing"*.

THE POWER OF FERVENT PRAYER
James 5:16-18

"The prayer of a righteous person has great power as it is working. 17 Elijah was a man with a nature like ours, and he prayed fervently that it might not rain, and for three years and six months it did not rain on the earth. 18 Then he prayed again, and heaven gave rain, and the earth bore its fruit."

Next, we are shown an example of the power of fervent prayer from the life of the prophet Elijah. It is interesting to learn that this powerful prophet was a man with a nature just like ours. He was not some superhuman person without flaws and weaknesses. He was a flawed human being just like you and me. However, his prayers were powerful because he was strong in faith and persistent in prayer.

In this context Elijah is given as an example of the power of a righteous person's prayers to God. Earlier we learned of the power of prayer when we make supplications, when we pray for the sick, and when we sin. Now we will confirm this truth with a powerful example from the life of Elijah.

Elijah prayed fervently. This word means, *"immensely passionate, hot or glowing, intense heat"*. Elijah was passionate in his prayers that it might not rain in Israel. Why? Surely he had in mind the Covenant of Blessing and Cursing that is found in Deuteronomy 28:1-30:20. This covenant specifically said that if Israel were unfaithful to God the ground would become hard like, *"bronze, and the earth under you shall be iron. The LORD will make the rain of your land powder. From heaven dust shall come down on you until you are destroyed,"* Deuteronomy 28:23-24.

Elijah's fervent prayer was that God would bring such a drought upon Israel because of their disobedience. The Bible tells us that Ahab, *"did evil in the sight of the LORD, more than all who were before him,"* 1 Kings 16:30. As a result the people were led astray to worship the Baal god instead of Jehovah God. They needed a drought in order to bring them back to God. Because of his fervency in prayer and his faith in God, Elijah was able to go to Ahab to inform him there would be no rain except by his word. Therefore, there was no rain for three years and six months. That is an extremely powerful prayer!

Read 1 Kings 18:1-46. The passage tells the events leading up to the end of the drought. Elijah held a competition between himself and 500 prophets of Baal. In the end the false prophets failed the test and were put to death. I especially like the section where Elijah goes to a high place and prays for rain seven times. The first time there was not even a cloud in the sky. This process continued seven times. I wonder how many of us would have prayed more than two or three times before we gave up in despair? After the seventh time all he saw was a cloud about the size of a man's fist. The prophet told his servant, *"Go up, say to Ahab, 'Prepare your chariot and go down, lest the rain stop you,"* 1 Kings 18:44. How is that for faith in God to answer prayer?

Elijah's personal response was to gather up his garments (some translations say, to gird up your loins) and run towards the city of Samaria to beat the rain. Girding up the loins was when a man wearing a long flowing robe would gather it up between his legs and tie it off so he could work in the field. In Elijah's case, he did so in order to run to the city to beat the rain. The text tells us, *"In a little while the heavens grew black with clouds and wind, and there was a great rain,"* 1 Kings 18:45. Once the rains came, the earth was watered, the plants were nourished and the earth once again bore fruit. How is that for a blessing wrought because of fervent prayer?

We have more power in our prayers than anyone can imagine. Jesus said, *"If you have faith and do not doubt, you will not only do what has been done to the fig tree, but even if you say to this mountain, be taken up and thrown into the sea, it will happen. And whatever you ask in prayer, you will receive, if you have faith,"* Matthew 21:21-23. A strong faith, fervent prayers, and a powerful God make for great results. We can *"do all things through him who strengthens me,"* Philippians 4:13.

HINDERANCES TO PRAYER

While we are on the topic of prayer, please consider some things that will hinder our prayers and make them ineffective.

Praying with improper motives. If we fail to ask, our prayers will be hindered, James 4:2. When we ask for the wrong reasons, God will not hear our prayers, James 4:3. Go back to our study of those passages to see how our prayers can be hindered when we do not have the correct motives.

Praying while in rebellion to God. That is, while walking in sinful ways. *"Your iniquities have made a separation between you and your God, and your sins have hidden his face from you so that he does not hear,"* Isaiah 59:2. It is not that God cannot hear a sinner's prayer; it is that He will not hear. The Lord will only forgive sin when a person comes to God acknowledging his sin and asking for forgiveness.

Prayers by couples who do not respect each other, 1 Peter 3:1-7. This verse begins by commanding wives to respect their husbands and to win them over by their godly conduct. Then, the verse commands husbands to live with their wives in an understanding way showing them honor. Mutual respect between couples is essential to an effective prayer life. Without it our prayers will definitely be hindered.

Praying to God when one is serving an idol. *"Son of man, these men have taken their idols into their hearts, and set the stumbling block of their iniquity before their faces. Should I indeed let myself be consulted by them?"* Ezekiel 14:3. God hates idolatry and will punish all who worship them. When we think of idols we probably think of images made by men's hands but, according to Colossians 3:5 and Ephesians 5:5, covetousness is also idolatry. Thus, we understand that anything we put in the place that belongs to God becomes our idol. Idolatrous practices will hinder our prayers.

When we love sinful practices, *"If I had cherished iniquity in my heart, the Lord would not have listened,"* Psalm 66:18. Whatever you cherish will dominate your life. That is why we are to love God with all our being and to love our neighbor as our self, Matthew 22:34-40. Far too many human beings love iniquity. If that is the case, their prayers will not be heard.

When we fail to confess our sins, James 5:16; 1 John 1:8-2:2. It is not enough to be aware of your sin. You must also experience godly grief that leads to sorrow for sin. Forgiveness leads to reformation of life. Godly repentance will lead to salvation, 2 Corinthians 7:9. However, a failure to confess your sins will definitely hinder your prayers.

Prayer is such an important part of the Christian's life. It is good for us to study the topic and realize how powerful and important a good prayer life is to the believer. It is also important to see some of the things that will hinder our prayers. Once we get it right, then, *"We know that he hears us in whatever we ask."* If He hears us, *"we know that we have the requests that we have asked of him,"* 1 John 5:15. Never forget, *"The prayer of a righteous person has great power as it is working,"* James 5:16.

THOSE WHO WANDER AWAY
James 5:19-20

*"My brothers, if anyone among you wanders from the truth and someone brings him back, *[20]* let him know that whoever brings back a sinner from his wandering will save his soul from death and will cover a multitude of sins."*

James concludes his book by calling us to seek out those who have fallen away from the truth and to bring them back to faithfulness. In the context some of those who were previously faithful brothers had <u>wandered away</u> from the truth and had become sinners. They needed to be brought back to faithfulness. This is yet another verse of scripture that proves a faithful believer in Jesus Christ can wander away and be lost. However, if faithful brethren go to them and bring them back they can be restored to faithfulness.

A believer could not wander away from the truth if he had never been in it in the first place. Therefore, this passage speaks of a believer who will be lost unless he comes back to the truth he once professed.

FIRST JEWEL: A believer can wander away and be lost. There are many who believe a person who is truly saved cannot fall away but the Bible does not support this teaching. Do you see the progression presented in James 5:19-20? 1) They are brothers. 2) They wander from the truth. 3) They are brought back to faithfulness. 4) Their soul is saved from death. 5) A multitude of sins are covered. The sins that are covered belonged to those who wandered away and were brought back to faithfulness. Heaven is filled with joy when a sinner repents and comes back to the Lord, Luke 15:7.

Study the following verses to learn that a believer could sin in such a way that would cause him to lose his salvation:

From Galatians. *"You are severed from Christ, you who would be justified by the law; you have fallen away from grace,"* Galatians 5:4. Everyone who has received the grace of God through faith is saved. In this passage we learn that if we go back to our former beliefs (in this case, back to the Law of Moses) we will be severed from Christ. You cannot be severed from Christ unless you were first attached to Him. Paul says such a person has *"fallen away from grace"*. You cannot fall from grace unless you first received it. Therefore, such a person, if he continues on the wrong path, will be lost. He was once saved, but now he is lost. He has fallen from grace. A believer can wander away from the truth and be lost.

From 2 Peter. *"For if, after they have escaped the defilements of the world through the knowledge of our Lord and Savior Jesus Christ, they are again entangled in them and overcome, the last state has become worse for them than the first. For it would have been better for them never to have known the way of righteousness than after knowing it to turn back from the holy commandments delivered to them. What the true proverb says has happened to them, 'The dog returns to its own vomit, and the sow after washing herself, returns to wallow in the mire,'"* 2 Peter 2:20-22. This passage speaks of a believer who has gone back to his former way of life. Because he turned back his salvation has been lost and he is worse off than he was before he first believed. No wonder the word of God encourages us to be faithful until death. A believer can wander away from the truth and be lost. Don't let it happen to you!

SECOND JEWEL: We are our brother's keeper. You know the story of Cain and Abel, Genesis 4. Cain killed his brother and when God asked him where his brother was he replied, *"Am I my brother's keeper?"* Genesis 4:9. The Lord places a burden upon each of us who believe to seek out those of our number who wander away and try to bring them back to faithful service. In doing so, we bring a sinner back from his wandering ways and we save his soul from death. The repentance of the fallen Christian will cover a multitude of sins. That is, his sins. When he repents and comes back to the Lord it will be as if he never sinned.

"Jewels from James" is now finished. It is my prayer that you have been built up in your faith by your study of the book of James. I also pray that your study of this great epistle is not over but that you will continue to glean more precious *"jewels"* as you continue to study the word. I am convinced that studying the book of James (and the entire Bible) will help us to become better servants of God and our Lord Jesus Christ. To God be the glory both now and forever!

DISCUSSION QUESTIONS:

1. Discuss the five *"jewels"* discussed under **PRAYER IS A WAY OF LIFE**, James 5:13-17. Which areas do you need to strengthen in your own prayer life?

   Discuss **THE POWER OF EFFECTIVE PRAYER**, James 5:16. Talk about ways to be more powerful in your own prayer life

2. Discuss the power of Elijah from 1 Kings 18:1-46.

3. Discuss the hindrances to prayer listed in this chapter.

4. Discuss James 5:19-20. Talk about wandering away, a faithful brother who wanders away, and talk about a multitude of sins being forgiven.

5. Whose responsibility is it to bring the wanderer back to faithfulness? Discuss ways this can be accomplished.

6. Discuss forgiveness. Include the difference between God forgiving a person and the forgiveness we give to each other. Is it the samethe same?

Made in the USA
Middletown, DE
14 May 2018